THE STORY OF OUR LANGUAGE

HENRY ALEXANDER received his education at the universities of Liverpool and Oxford. He has been professor of English language and head of the department of English at Queen's University, Kingston, Ontario, and has taught at Oxford, Harvard, Toronto, Uppsala University in Sweden, and the Linguistic Institute of America. For many years he lectured at and directed the summer school for non-English-speaking students at Queen's University and has done field work for the Linguistic Atlas of the United States and Canada in the Maritime Provinces of eastern Canada. Besides a number of articles on linguistic subjects which have appeared in periodicals in England, Canada, the United States and Europe, Dr. Alexander has written two books, *The Place Names of Oxfordshire* and *Common Faults in Writing English.* He has also translated many books from the Scandinavian languages, including two volumes of plays by the eighteenth-century Danish dramatist Holberg.

Dr. Alexander, who is a Fellow of the Royal Society of Canada, is now retired and living in London.

The Story of Our Language

Henry Alexander

Dolphin Books
Doubleday & Company, Inc.
Garden City, New York

Doubleday & Co.
Garden City

Contents

CONTENTS

Preface

The writer of a short history of the language is faced with several difficulties. Should he restrict the subject-matter to one or two aspects of linguistic development, mainly vocabulary, or should he attempt, even at the risk of superficiality, to describe the various directions in which a language shows change—sounds, forms, syntax and meaning? The latter course seems essential if the book is to justify its title. This plan requires the inclusion of a certain amount of material that is somewhat technical, in addition to the discussion of such topics as vocabulary and change of meaning, which lend themselves to a more lively treatment. But the reader who wishes to obtain a picture of the processes that our language has undergone in different periods will need this information; the reader who is less eager for a comprehensive view will no doubt follow Chaucer's advice and

Turne over the leef and chese [choose] another tale.

A second problem lies in the question of phonetic notation. Certain portions of this book—for instance, the explanation of "the great vowel shift"—would have been easier to write and easier to read, for those acquainted with phonetics, if a phonetic alphabet had been used. It is not safe, however, to assume this knowledge, and as a preliminary discussion of phonetic theory and phonetic symbols would have unduly increased the size of the book and perhaps discouraged the general reader, it was decided, after much hesitation, to submit to the limitations of the ordinary alphabet.

In a region so well explored as the history of the English language it is difficult to stake any new claims. I fear that there are no fresh discoveries in this book; the only personal contribution is perhaps the synthesis and a few modern instances. Like all writers on the subject, I am deeply indebted to the great pioneer works in the field, especially to the Oxford Dictionary, that rich storehouse of accurate knowledge. Its abundant resources have been freely used in compiling material for several chapters of this book. In addition, many works on the same subject and on general linguistics have provided ideas and illustrations.

It is a pleasure to thank several friends and colleagues who read parts of the original version of the book either in MS. or in proof. These include Dr. A. R. Jewitt, Dr. H. Kurath (who kindly read the chapters on American English), Dr. H. Kökeritz, Dr. J. Vincent.

THE STORY OF OUR LANGUAGE

1.   Our Changing Language

Few subjects give rise to so much discussion as questions
of usage in language. Should road-signs read *Drive slow*
or *Drive slowly* or avoid the issue by *Proceed with caution?*
Shall we pronounce the *t* in *often?* Is *schedule* to have the
sound of *sh–* or *sk–?* Is *(n)either* to be pronounced
(n)eyether or *(n)eether?* Is it right to say *I have gotten* as
well as *I have got?* Are we declassed if we pronounce the
past tense of *eat* as *et?* Are the North American terms
movie, radio, gas(oline) preferable to the British *cinema,
wireless, petrol?* The list could be extended almost indefi-
nitely, and at some time or other most people have argued
about these or similar points. They give rise to much strong
feeling, perhaps only equalled by differences in religion
and politics. On one occasion in biblical times the pronunciation of the word *shibboleth* was literally a matter
of life and death.[1] We do not go so far now, but a tone
of bitterness often enters into discussions of what seem
harmless problems. The reason is, of course, that, con-
sciously or unconsciously, we attach social values to the
question of speech. The North American who pronounces
the past tense of *eat* to rime with *fate* looks down on the
speaker who uses *et*, in spite of the fact that most British
people, including no doubt royalty and aristocracy and the
hierarchy of the church, generally say *et*. The devotee of
et, on the contrary, thinks that the other form is the mark
of a purist or a pedant. The same holds good for *of(t)en*;
those who sound the *t* think the *t*-less speaker is careless,

[1] Judges, XII, 6.

13

perhaps vulgar; the advocates of *offen* accuse their opponents of being slaves to spelling and ask them, not without some reason, if they pronounce the *t* in *Christmas, whistle* or *listen.*

It seldom occurs to those who argue about these matters to look into the history of the word or phrase in question. If they did so, they might often find some help. Not that a problem of modern usage can be settled altogether by an appeal to the past; it does not follow that because a certain form of speech was current in earlier times it is therefore acceptable today—we might as well suggest that, because in Queen Elizabeth's time our forefathers dressed in doublet and hose, we could wear the same garb without causing excitement and suspicion as to our mental condition. But the appeal to history is one factor that may occasionally aid us in arriving at a decision —it gives us the background of a modern locution—and it will at least tell us how the various forms originated. Such an appeal will immediately convince us of one important fact that is fundamental if we are to have a correct attitude towards language—namely, that our speech is continually changing, that the language of one generation is never quite the same as that of another, and that these factors of change and development must be considered in any judgment we arrive at about present-day usage.

If we are observant we can easily detect this process of continuous linguistic change all around us. We do not speak quite in the same way as our parents, certainly not as our grandparents. The younger generation will often shock their elders by the terms they use and even by their pronunciation, just as their elders, when they were young, disturbed their parents or grandparents. Thus, for instance, the garment formerly called *trousers* is rapidly becoming *pants* in the colloquial speech of North America, perhaps a regrettable tendency, but one that cannot be ignored; the older generation, however, still generally prefers the more dignified word. The garment that people used to call *waistcoat* (often pronounced *weskit*) is now generally *vest*. One can occasionally hear in the speech of elderly people, especially in rural districts, the older term *wristbands* (pronounced *rizbans*) instead of *cuffs*. A *tie* was formerly a *necktie*, even a *cravat*. These are only four examples taken from one department in our vocabulary, the names for articles of clothing; an examination of other groups of words denoting familiar objects and ideas would show similar changes. In pronunciation the same holds good. The word *forehead*, generally pronounced nowadays as *fore+head*, was formerly *forid* or *fored*, a pronunciation that may still be heard from older speakers, perhaps more frequently in England than in North America. Not very long ago the word *forward* had much the same sound (*forard*), and this is still preserved as a kind of linguistic fossil in the speech of sailors. More instances of this process can easily be found.

If we can detect this amount of divergence arising in the course of one or two generations, the changes would obviously be much greater over a period of several centuries. In fact, if we could be transported by a time-machine back to the age of Shakespeare, we might have some difficulty in understanding the spoken English of his day; it is even more probable that Shakespeare would not understand our English. If, instead of going back some 350 years to Shakespeare's age, we went back about 550 years to Chaucer's time we should have still more difficulty. A final journey of a thousand years into the past would bring us to a language that we could not understand at all; although the ancestor of modern English, it would be almost as remote from our present-day speech as French, Latin or German. We should also find that the rate of change was much greater in the past than in more recent times. This is not difficult to explain. In early times language was primarily something spoken—this is still true, though not to the same extent. Speech is a form of human activity and, like every other human activity, is subject to change and modification. It is not more surprising to find changes in our speech than, let us say, in our fashions in dress or our methods of dancing, which we can see developing new features from year to year. Speech, which reflects life, has to keep pace with life, a fact which purists seem to forget. But in modern times we have paid more attention to the written language, to books and printed matter. This form of language is more stable than the spoken word. It acts as a brake. In an age when practically everyone can read or write rapid change is consequently checked. We may note, however, that, with the widespread use of radio, films and television, the spoken language seems once more to be coming into its own; it is possible that, as a result, the rate of change in speech may increase. Another factor which slows up change in language is the school. The teacher is inclined, as a rule, to discourage innovations in usage. He has acquired a certain set of speech habits and, in his turn, he hands them on to his pupils. Thus in an age when education and books are widespread we become more conservative in our speech. The teacher and the printing-press are the great supporters of linguistic tradition.

Variation in language shows itself in many different ways; it may be due, among other causes, to the factors of space or time or, indeed, to a combination of both. The striking differences between North American and British English have been produced chiefly by the obstacle of three thousand miles of ocean which prevents easy communication and the circulation of words and phrases between countries on different sides of the Atlantic. Radio, TV and films help greatly to break down this barrier of distance, but do not entirely succeed. The few examples already given of words that differ in the two forms of speech could easily be increased. Sometimes the British word is quite unfamiliar in North America; sometimes the American word needs explanation to the Englishman. Few people in England, for instance, would know the meaning of *bleachers* or a *campus* or a *shiv*; few people in North America could be sure of what the Englishman means when he talks about the *bonnet* of his car or a *lay-by* (parking space off the highway) or a *batman* (officer's servant). It would be easy to draw up a long list of terms such as *radio, wireless; candies, sweets; thumbtacks* (or *pushpins*), *drawing-pins; a spool of thread, a reel of cotton*—modes of expression which change as we cross the Atlantic and which sometimes cause embarrassment to the traveller.

The changes caused by time are just as easy to detect. The most important are changes in sounds, in spelling, in the forms and meaning of words, and in syntax, that is, the arrangement of words in phrases and sentences.

CHANGES IN SOUND

Many changes in sounds are indicated by modifications in the spelling. When we find our modern words *bone, home, oak* written *ban, ham, ac* a thousand years ago, *boon, hoom, ook* six hundred years ago, we may be sure that their pronunciation has changed during the ages. Sometimes the spelling does not reflect this change so clearly, and we have to look for other evidence. One of the most useful tests is that of rime. Thus, for instance, when Pope (1688–1744) writes

> Yet write, O write me all, that I may *join*
> Griefs to my griefs, and echo sighs to *thine*

in a poem (*Eloisa to Abelard*) in which every two lines rime, it is evident that one of the words *join, thine* could not have been pronounced as it is today. This and other facts show that the word *join* was pronounced in Pope's day—and even rather earlier—something like *jine*, a pronunciation that has not yet completely disappeared. But in normal speech *join* now has the sound of *oy* in *boy*. This sound-change, caused by the influence of the spelling *oi*, must therefore have taken place in relatively recent times.

Another illustration may be given from the same writer. In *The Rape of the Lock* we find the following couplets:

> Soft yielding minds to water glide *away*
> And sip, with Nymphs, their elemental *tea*.
> Here thou, great Anna! whom three realms *obey*,
> Dost sometimes counsel take—and sometimes *tea*.

In Pope's day these lines contained a good rime because *tea* was pronounced something like *tay*; here, again, the old pronunciation can still occasionally be heard today, especially among Irish speakers, but in more general speech the word has developed the same sound as in *see*. Examination of other earlier poems, even sometimes as late as the nineteenth century, will yield further examples.

CHANGES IN SPELLING AND FORMS

Spelling shows many changes, though, for reasons already mentioned, they are far fewer in modern than in earlier times. If we were to read Shakespeare in the spelling of his own age and not in a normalized modern edition, we should find considerable variation from our present-day spelling. Thus the first page of *Hamlet* in the quarto edition of 1603 has such spellings as *tragicall, historie, meete, leegemen, souldier, releeved, peece, seene, sayes, fantasie, wil, beliefe, centinels*—all in the first twenty lines.

If we go back to Chaucer we find *koude* (could), *condicioun* (condition), *ooth* (oath), *seyd* (said), *contree*, *armee* (country, army), and so on. Sometimes his spellings are better, because they are closer to the pronunciation, than our modern ones. Thus *koude* without its silent and unhistorical *l* is a better spelling than *could*, and the *c* in *condicioun* is a better attempt to show the sound than our *t*. In many cases, of course, these earlier spellings represent different sounds from those found in the corresponding words today, and so the variants reflect a change both of spelling and of sound.

The forms of Chaucer's words, even sometimes of Shakespeare's, often differ from ours. Thus Chaucer has such plurals as *eyen, toon, foon* for *eyes, toes, foes*. He often has a prefix *y–* in the past participle of a verb, e.g. *yfallen*, or an ending *–en* in the infinitive, e.g. *riden* or *ryden*, 'to ride'. Some of these features will be found in Spenser, writing two hundred years later, though here they are often deliberate attempts to be old-fashioned. But even Shakespeare's forms often deviate from our modern English usage, for instance, *writ* for *written* or *wrote*, *spoke* for *spoken*, *forgot* for *forgotten*, *hid* for *hidden*, *catch'd* for *caught*, *worser* for *worse*, *county* for *count*. If Shakespeare writes *I have took*[2] or *Have you chose*[3] we must not accuse him of ignorance of English grammar; the explanation is merely that in these forms, as in so many others, literary usage has become more stable since his day.

CHANGES IN MEANING

When Shakespeare writes in *King Lear*:

> But mice, and rats, and such small *deer*

[2] *Julius Caesar*, II, 1.50.
[3] *Coriolanus*, II, 3.163.

it is obvious that he is not using *deer* in its modern meaning, but that it is equivalent here to *animals*. This, as we shall see later, was the earlier significance of the word, and its change from a general to a more restricted meaning illustrates a common linguistic process. Another clear instance of a difference in meaning will be seen in the word *nice*:

> Romeo, that spoke him fair, bade him bethink
> How *nice* the quarrel was.

From this and other similar passages it appears that Shakespeare used *nice* in the sense of *foolish, trifling,* sometimes also in the sense of *exact.* The observant reader will have no difficulty in collecting more examples of similar changes in meaning from any early writer. Note, for instance, the usual meanings attached in Shakespeare's writings to such words as *fond, naughty, presently, humour.*

CHANGES IN SYNTAX

If, instead of looking at isolated words, we examine the way in which words are combined in phrases and sentences, or syntax, the same process of gradual change will be noticed. Nowadays, for instance, it is considered incorrect to have two or more negatives in a sentence; such a phrase as *He can't find nobody nowhere* has become the sign of an uneducated speaker. This is a comparatively recent development in English, and again we have only to look at Shakespeare's work to find that in his day it was quite permissible. Thus in *Romeo and Juliet* we read:

> I will *not* budge for *no* man's pleasure, I.

In Chaucer we can find as many as four negatives in one sentence. In speaking of the Knight in the *Canterbury Tales* he says:

He *nevere* yet *no* vilenye *ne* seyde
In al his lyf unto *no* maner wight.

This, if translated literally, would run: he *never* did *not* say *no* harm to *no* kind of creature in all his life. There is a sentence in the Anglo-Saxon version of Bede's Latin *Ecclesiastical History* which, if rendered literally into modern English, would read: He could *not never* make *no* falsehood *nor* idle song.[4] In former times the psychological effect of piling up negatives was to gain emphasis; the more negatives, the stronger became the idea of negation. This may still be true in popular speech today. But in more educated language logic has prevailed, and we accept the idea that two negatives generally cancel each other and make an affirmative. As a result, this older syntactical feature is disappearing.

Another curious feature of Shakespearian syntax unknown in modern English is the so-called "ethic dative". It too was a device to gain emphasis. A well-known example is seen in a line from *The Taming of the Shrew*:

Villain, knock *me* at the gate.

This might be explained as: "Knock at the gate *for me*", but Shakespeare's construction is impossible today. It is not a mere "poetic licence". We can find it also in prose, e.g. "Thou art like one of those fellows that when he enters the confines of a tavern claps *me* his sword upon the table" (*Romeo and Juliet*). In this sentence *me* is not equivalent to *for me*; it is purely rhetorical; in modern English it might be: He claps his sword on the table, *you know*.

These are only two out of many examples of syntactical change. Many more could be added, especially with regard to the order of words in the sentence. In modern English the pattern is very stable, in affirmative sentences gen-

[4] he . . . *naefre noht* leasunge *ne* idles leoðes wyrcan *ne* meahte.

erally subject + verb + object, e.g. *The man hit the dog*. But in earlier English this order was by no means so regular; the verb often came at the end of the sentence. Questions and commands also show considerable differences. *What say you?* has become *What do you say?*; *Tell not me* is now *Do not tell me*. This also illustrates how the use of auxiliaries such as *do* has affected the structure of the English sentence.

From this brief survey two points emerge that are fundamental if we are to understand the nature and the history of any language. First, we must not expect a language, at any stage in its development, to show a uniform pattern; absolute regularity in speech exists only in the minds of rigid purists. Language was made for man and not man for language; it is a tool that he has forged and has to use in his own way. Secondly, changes are normal and inevitable in all departments of language. These facts were recognized, though they were not always approved of, by earlier writers. Thus Caxton, writing towards the end of the fifteenth century, says: "And certaynly our langage now used varyeth ferre from that whiche was used and spoken when I was borne. For we englysshe men ben borne under the domynacyon of the mone, which is never stedfaste, but ever waverynge, wexynge one season, and waneth and dyscreaseth another season." And Chaucer, a century earlier, records the lack of uniformity in the English of his day:

> And, for there is so gret diversite
> In English and in writing of our tonge.

The story of a language presents a picture of prevailing tendencies, a connected account of past changes, and an attempt to show why these have occurred.

2. Some Features of Modern English

Before describing the earliest stages of English and tracing its development down to the present day, it will be useful to point out certain striking features of modern English. To begin a history at the end may seem a paradox, but we can build up a picture of older English more easily if we have beforehand a concrete idea of what our language is like today, especially in comparison with foreign tongues. Few people have made this examination; we inherit our speech without any great effort, and we are seldom obliged to look at it objectively as a foreigner has to do and note its outstanding characteristics. In many respects English is unique among modern languages; it has developed along very special lines.

If we compare English with modern languages such as French or German or ancient languages such as Latin or Greek, we notice at once the simplicity of its grammar, especially in the endings or inflections of words. Take, for instance, the adjective. In modern English this has only one form—*good*, *beautiful*, etc.—except of course for the comparative and superlative, where we often add *-er* or *-est*. But we can say *a good man, a good woman, a good road, good men, women, roads* without any change in the word *good*. This cannot be done in most other European languages. In French we must change *bon* to *bonne* if the noun is feminine, to *bons* or *bonnes* if the noun is plural; thus we find four forms where we have only one in English. French *beau* is even more complex; here we have *beau, bel, belle, beaux, belles* according to the noun that

23

follows—five forms instead of one. German has also five different forms for the adjective, while, if we go back to an ancient language like Latin, we discover no less than fifteen. In the oldest stage of English the adjective had numerous endings; this is one of the many cases where we have discarded an elaborate linguistic pattern.

The word *the* shows an equally striking simplicity. Here French has *le*, *la*, *l'*, *les* and many combinations with prepositions such as *du*, *de la*, *de l'*, *des*, *au*, *à la*, *à l'*, *aux*, where in English *the* never varies. In German we find six different forms. Here again English formerly showed the same variation; at one time *the* had at least a dozen different forms. Once more we have travelled from complexity to simplicity.

A glance at the verb reveals the same contrast, though the simplifying process has not gone quite so far. Here is the conjugation of the present tense of a verb in English, French and Latin:

I come	je	vien-*s*	ven-*io*
you come	tu	vien-*s*	ven-*is*
he come-*s*	il	vien-*t*	ven-*it*
we come	nous	ven-*ons*	ven-*imus*
you come	vous	ven-*ez*	ven-*itis*
they come	ils	vienn-*ent*	ven-*iunt*

It will be noticed that while English has only one ending —the *s* of *comes*—French has five and Latin six. Note also the change in the root of the French verb. It is true that the Latin inflections help to show the person and number, so that, if we choose, we may omit the pronouns in Latin, but the difference is still very marked. The same comparison would hold good for other tenses of the verb. Another radical development in modern English is the almost complete disappearance of the subjunctive mood, which provides us with an extra set of forms in French and Latin.

Everyone who has struggled with the subjunctive in these two languages will appreciate this simplification. In English it is only retained in such fossilized phrases as *if I were, if he were, if it be;* this does not, however, involve any new forms, as both *were* and *be* are already familiar to us because of their use in other parts of the verbal system.

The noun shows a parallel process of reduction, as will be seen later. There is not so much difference between the amount of inflection in the English and French nouns, but a comparison between the declensions of the noun in English and Latin reveals the same contrast as has been shown in other parts of speech. While English has not yet gone so far as Chinese, which has no inflections at all, it has proceeded a considerable distance in that direction.

In one respect, however, English has become more instead of less complex. That is in the system of tenses in the verb. Again a glance at French or Latin will show the contrast. In translating the present tense of a French or Latin verb we have at least three possibilities in English; thus *j'aime* or *amo* may be rendered as *I love, I am loving,* or *I do love.* All three are forms of the present tense, but obviously each carries a slightly different signification. By this device English can be more exact; by a simple method it can indicate fine shades of meaning, which are often of importance. In this case, therefore, a richer grammatical apparatus seems to be justified.

Lastly, one other important and indeed revolutionary feature is seen in English which sets it apart from most other European languages, both modern and ancient. In Latin, French, German we have what is called grammatical gender, that is, a word is masculine, feminine, or neuter, not because it denotes a male or female being or an inanimate object or abstract idea, but simply because in the remote past some conventional gender has been attached to the word. Thus in French the word *table* is feminine, while the word *pupitre* (desk) is masculine. In German we have a still stranger situation; the word *Kind* (child) is neuter, even the word for woman (*Weib*) is neuter. Latin shows the same phenomenon: *mensa* (table) is feminine, *murus* (wall) is masculine, *iter* (journey) is neuter. The earliest form of English had the same feature. But in our present-day speech a male person or animal is masculine, referred to as *he* or *him*, a female is feminine (*she* or *her*), and an inanimate object or an abstraction is neuter (*it*). There are a few exceptions; a ship and a country are often indicated by *she* and *her* because they are personified, but usually the rule holds good. In modern English we have logical and not grammatical gender.

Before leaving these features of English there is one point to be emphasized, even at the risk of being accused of propaganda. It is often maintained that the elaborate grammatical apparatus of French and German, and still more of Latin and Greek, makes these languages supremely logical and therefore superior to a less complex language like our own. This view is difficult to accept. What, after all, is the test of a language? Surely its adequacy as a means of communication; if it enables us to express our ideas and emotions effectively it is a good medium, no matter how simple its structure. Now do the French or Latin inflections improve the clarity of these languages? Is English, with its one adjectival form *good*, any poorer as a means of communication than these other languages with their numerous forms that have continually to be changed to suit the accompanying noun? Or do the variations of the definite article in French and German add anything to the meaning that cannot be expressed just as exactly and adequately by the one English word *the?* Is the threefold repetition of the possessive ending in the Latin (*pater*) du*arum* bon*arum* puell*arum* any improvement on our phrase (*the father*) *of the two good girls*, where the idea of possession is indicated once for all by the simple word *of?* Is a Latin clause with *cum* and the subjunctive any clearer than an English clause with *when* and no subjunctive? It is hard to find any real basis for these claims; in fact one is tempted to suggest that the great mass of inflections in modern and ancient languages is unnecessary baggage which the language has to carry. English prefers to travel lightly; it gets to its destination just as well, and sometimes, like the lightly-burdened traveller, rather more comfortably and rapidly. In one respect at least, the absence of grammatical gender, English is definitely more logical than most other languages. Most modern linguists have discarded the idea that a highly complex system of inflections is in itself a virtue; if they try to assess the relative merits of different languages their attitude is a pragmatic one: that language is superior which works best in practice, which enables us to communicate with our fellow men briefly, clearly and, if the occasion demands it, with appropriate emotional overtones. In spite of—perhaps because of—the simplicity of its formal pattern English certainly achieves these aims.

In striking contrast, however, to this simplicity are the wealth and variety of our modern vocabulary. Here, possibly, there is ground for criticism. We have almost too many words in present-day English. Beginning with a relatively small stock of words, we have gradually added to these by many different processes which will be discussed later, until now we are almost overwhelmed. It has been estimated that there are nearly half a million words in English today. Many of these are latent; nobody ever uses them; and the active everyday vocabulary of even the most erudite and eloquent speaker is a small fraction of this figure. Much of our vocabulary consists of what we may call "learned" words; the proportion of these is greater than in most other languages because of the way we have obtained our new words. In this respect there is a great contrast between English and German. While German tends to coin its new words out of its own speech-material,[1] adopting a kind of linguistic nationalism, we prefer generally to go outside English and borrow words from other languages, both ancient and modern. Thus, in the course of time, as we shall see, almost every known tongue has contributed something to our ever-increasing store of words. The English vocabulary is a mosaic. A simple illustration will show the contrast between the English and the German method of word-coinage. When the telephone was invented and a new word was needed for a new object, the Germans put together two native German words, *fern* (far) and *Sprecher* (speaker) and thus made a new compound *Fernsprecher*, literally "far-speaker", parallel to our "loud-speaker". English, on the other hand, went beyond the boundaries of the language and combined two words of Greek origin, *tele* (far) and *phone* (sound), thus building up a new compound out of non-English speech-material. In this case there was no difficulty in the interpretation of the word, because the object it denoted is so well-known that people soon became familiar with the new term. But with less ordinary objects, and especially with abstracts, the English habit of building up words from Greek and Latin does often constitute a real obstacle for those who have not studied these languages, and the German method is far easier for the comparatively uneducated reader. How many people who are unfamiliar with classical languages can be sure of the meaning of

---

[1] It is true that German has also borrowed words, mainly from French, but these are generally of a simpler type than many of the English words coined from Latin and Greek.

such words as *adumbrate, pusillanimous, peregrination, ubiquitous, retrograde, epigram, repercussion,* etc.? This element in our vocabulary has encouraged a form of humour, more common in English than other languages, which arises from the distortion of words. It is sometimes called *malapropism,* after the greatest perpetrator of these mistakes, Mrs. Malaprop in Sheridan's play *The Rivals,* who reached her highest achievement in this direction when she talked of "a nice derangement of epitaphs" (arrangement of epithets). From Shakespeare's Dame Quickly, his nurse in *Romeo and Juliet,* Quince and Bottom, down to some present-day comic strips, this has been a perennial comic device. A dictionary is probably more of a household necessity to English-speaking people than to the people of other nations. Because it contains so many words which are not immediately intelligible to ordinary readers, English has been called, with some justice, an undemocratic language.[2] By following the doctrine of free trade and unrestricted imports in our vocabulary we have been blessed with abundant resources; it is possible that a mild linguistic tariff would have been beneficial. On the other hand, it may be argued that we are not compelled to use these words. We can certainly express ideas of great nobility and profundity without them. If, for instance, we look at Wordsworth's famous lines,

> To me the meanest flower that blows can give
> Thoughts that do often lie too deep for tears,

we see that only the simplest words are used; in fact only three words have more than one syllable. Much of our finest literature is written with equal simplicity. Shakespeare can be just as effective with the same elemental vocabulary, e.g.

[2] Jespersen, *Growth and Structure of the English Language,* p. 143.

> We are such stuff
> As dreams are made on; and our little life
> Is rounded with a sleep.

Once more we find a fundamental philosophical statement enshrined in three lines of which only two words contain more than one syllable. Neither of these two writers, however, confines himself to this unadorned language. Shakespeare can write "the multitudinous seas incarnadine", and Wordsworth, addressing an infant, can say, in the poem already quoted:[3]

> Thou, whose exterior semblance doth belie
> Thy Soul's immensity.

An interesting attempt to counteract this excess of words is seen in Basic English, a scheme whereby 850 words alone are selected and used to express all ordinary ideas, with a small supplementary vocabulary for any specific science or technical subject. Surprising results have been obtained with this medium, and one frequently notices how much clearer a passage becomes when reduced to Basic than it is in orthodox English, where the overabundant vocabulary has led to looseness of thought and statement. As a method of introducing non-English speakers to the language Basic seems to have some merits, though some features of its structure, especially the almost complete absence of verbs, create difficulties in expression.

Finally, we may mention the defence sometimes put forward on behalf of the "learned" words in our language, that they help to pave the way for the student of classics. But to burden the vocabulary with masses of polysyllabic words for the sake of the relatively small proportion of people who study Latin and Greek does not seem a wise

[3] *Ode on Intimations of Immortality.*

procedure. It reminds us of an equally fallacious argument for retaining our chaotic English spelling—that it throws light on the history of English words. In both cases we are accepting a serious drawback in the language for the sake of a minor and indeed doubtful advantage. The whole question of a mixed *versus* a relatively homogeneous vocabulary is not an easy one to settle.

One other defect, much more serious, in present-day English is our spelling. In this we have gone backwards instead of progressing. Five hundred or a thousand years ago the language had a better system of spelling than today. But during the last few centuries, while the sounds of speech have changed considerably, the spelling has been only slightly modified and even then not always for the better. The result is a continually increasing lag between the spelling and the sounds it is supposed to represent. There is no need to give long lists of examples; we meet them all the time as we read and write. Few languages can show a pair of words which are identical in sound but have not a single letter in common; this can be seen in the two English words *ewe* and *you*. We are almost reminded of a "picture language" like Chinese, where each word has its special symbol or "character". This is an extreme example of the imperfections in English spelling, but we have only to think of our silent letters in such words as *write, right, wright, knight, calm, doubt, isle, island*, our chameleon-like *–ough* with its seven or eight pronunciations, our *ie* and *ei* spelling, and all the other irregularities on which teachers and children spend so much time and effort, to realize that orthography is one of the weakest points in the linguistic pattern of modern English. It is true that many groups of words do show a correspondence between sound and symbol, but even they break down occasionally; thus in the group with "short *a*" such as *bad, man, cab*, we encounter *plaid* with a new symbol for the same sound and *war* with a new sound for the same symbol. In the "long *a*" group (*name, safe, gate*) we find *have* spoiling the regular pattern, in the "short *i*" group (*did, him, sit*) we encounter *build, hymn,* and the rule about "long *i*" (*mine, pipe, rise*) does not apply to *give* or *style.* All the laws about English spelling seem made only to be broken. Many attempts at reform have been made, but the situation seems almost hopeless, mainly because of the inertia and conservatism of those who have learned to spell in the orthodox manner and are therefore against change. In American English a few alterations have been made, but they are not nearly far-reaching enough. Meanwhile many millions of people, compelled to memorize a frequently illogical spelling, spend time and energy that might well be devoted to subjects that are far better mental discipline or have real cultural value. Few of the arguments put forward in favour of our present spelling will bear analysis.[4]

These then are some of the outstanding features of modern English. Simplicity of form and inflection is combined with an almost too abundant vocabulary and an orthography that is frequently chaotic. There is a mixture of good and bad, but the good points predominate—our linguistic assets more than counterbalance our liabilities. This is proved by the rapid advance of English as a world language, though political and economic factors have also contributed. We must now travel back into the past and see how this picture compares with what we discover in earlier periods of the language.

[4] For a complete discussion of this subject see T. R. Lounsbury, *English Spelling and Spelling Reform,* and for a defence of our present spelling see Sir W. A. Craigie, *English Spelling, Its Rules and Reasons.*

3. The Three Periods of English: The Origin of English and Its Relation to Other Languages

In tracing the history of English it is convenient to distinguish three different periods. First, there is the earliest age, from the arrival of the English in Britain down to about 1100. This is usually called the Old English (O.E.) or Anglo-Saxon period. From 1100 to about 1500 we have Middle English (M.E.). Finally there is Modern English (Mod. E.) from 1500 to the present day. Although the migration of the English people from the Continent of Europe took place mainly in the fifth and sixth centuries, we have very few records of anything written in English before about the year 700, after which we find an unbroken sequence of documents from which the nature of the language can be seen. If we take 700 as our starting-point, and 1900, which is close enough to the present day, as our final date, we get a convenient division into three periods of 400 years each.[1]

O.E.	700–1100
M.E.	1100–1500
Mod. E.	1500–1900

The outstanding literary work of the O.E. period is the epic poem *Beowulf*, written about 700; the most important M.E. work is the poetry of Chaucer, who died in 1400; while in Mod. E., starting with Spenser and Shake-

---

[1] There is considerable difference of opinion about these dates. Some writers place the end of the O.E. period about 1150; some give 1450 as the end of M.E. See, further, p. 111.

speare in the sixteenth century, there is a continuous series of great writers down to our own day.

We must not imagine the change from one of these periods to the next as abrupt and sudden, that on a certain day or week people stopped speaking Old English and started to speak Middle English. The process was rather like passing from one county to another when travelling; there is little at any one moment to show the change, but after a time one finds oneself in a new region. The evolution of the language was always gradual and just as imperceptible as it is at the present day; in any age there must have been considerable overlapping between old and new, the older generation, more conservative, retaining the earlier forms of speech, the younger adopting innovations. Even in the work of an individual writer we can often find a mixture of old and new forms. It must also be borne in mind that these changes were largely unconscious; they were not due to any deliberate effort on the part of the speaker.

English is not the original language of England but, like the English people themselves, came over from the continent of Europe. We cannot say what was the first language in England; that lies far back in the mists of prehistory. But we do know that, before the arrival of the English people and their language, there had existed for several centuries a tongue belonging to quite a different family of languages, the Celtic group. This was spoken by the ancient Britons. During the Roman occupation of Britain (43–410) Latin must also have been widely used. Both these earlier languages, as we shall see, have left some traces on Old English. It was not until the middle of the fifth century, when the invading Teutonic tribes from the continent began to conquer the Britons and to impose on the country their own speech and social organization, that the history of the English language in England began. It had of course a long previous history on the continent, but to consider this would take us too far afield.

These continental tribes came from different parts of Northern Europe. Their exact origin is still an unsolved problem. With regard to two branches—the Angles and the Saxons—the historians are fairly well agreed; they came from a region around what is now Northern Germany. But in addition there was a third tribe, whose original home is less certain. These were the Jutes, who, according to the traditional view, migrated from Jutland, the northern part of Denmark; many modern historians, however, do not accept this explanation, which is based largely on the resemblance of the two names, Jutes and Jutland. The Angles settled mainly in the north and central portions of England and gave their name both to the country and its language; the Saxons settled mainly in the south; the Jutes in Kent, the south-eastern corner of England, and in the Isle of Wight. (See Map, p. 36). Mingled with these three main races there may well have been representatives of several other tribes, such as the Frisians, who inhabited what is now part of Holland, and even possibly the Franks.[2] Because of this mixed strain in the English people the term Anglo-Saxon is not quite accurate. To use Anglo-Saxon-Jute . . . etc. would be awkward; so the modern practice is to employ Old English to indicate this early stage of our language. This also has the advantage of being parallel to Middle English and Modern English and to the terminology applied to other languages, e.g. Old, Middle and Modern French. It also suggests the continuity of our language from its earliest stages. The Old English writers themselves used the term *englisc* or *engliscgereord*, "the English language". The use of "Anglo-

---

[2] See R. H. Hodgkin, *History of the Anglo-Saxons*, vol. 1, p. 97. This work is very valuable for the history of the early settlements.

Saxon" to indicate the English people and their language prior to the Norman Conquest arose at a relatively late period, in the 16th century.[3]

Before examining Old English and following its history and development we must indicate how it is related to other languages. One of the far-reaching discoveries of the 19th century was that many languages show important resemblances in their structure, and that these features are to be explained, not by a process of borrowing but by descent from a common ancestor. Languages are like plants or animals, which may differ considerably today but may still exhibit certain characteristics pointing to a common origin or parent stock. By grouping together those which show these similarities we are able to draw up various genera, families and classes. Languages, too, may be divided into families. To indicate a common descent for a group of languages or a group of words we use the term *cognate*. Some idea of the evidence on which these relationships are based may be obtained from the following facts.

Let us make a list of some common terms in several European languages and compare their appearance. We may take the first four numbers and the closest family relationships; many striking resemblances will emerge, which cannot be accidental.

English	German	Dutch	Swedish	Danish
one	ein	een	en	een
two	zwei	twee	två	to
	(German $z = ts$)			
three	drei	drie	tre	tre
four	vier	vier	fyra	fire
	(German $v = f$)			
father	vater ($v = f$)	vader	fader	fader
mother	mutter	moeder	moder	moder
brother	bruder	broeder	broder	broder
sister	schwester	zuster	syster	søster

[3] See *Shorter Oxford Dictionary* under *Anglo-Saxon*.

Notice also the pattern of the verbs:

	English	German	Dutch	Swedish	Danish
Infinitive	sing	singen	zingen	sjunga	synge
Past Tense	sang	sang	zong	sjöng	sang
Past Participle	sung	gesungen	gezongen	sjungit	sungen
	(O.E. gesungen)				
fish		fischen	visschen	fiska	fiske
fished	(–ed pron. t)	fischte	vischte	fiskade	fiskede
fished	" " "	gefischt	gevischt	fiskat	fisket

These and other similarities of an equally fundamental nature point to a common ancestry for this group of languages. They are called the Teutonic or Germanic group and are usually divided into three sub-groups, North Teutonic, East Teutonic and West Teutonic. All these are descended from one parent language, which is called Primitive Teutonic. The relationship can best be shown by the following table, which includes only the more important languages.

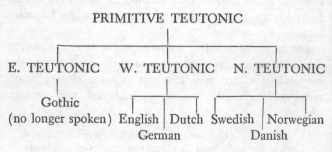

PRIMITIVE TEUTONIC

E. TEUTONIC   W. TEUTONIC   N. TEUTONIC

Gothic
(no longer spoken) English | Dutch Swedish | Norwegian
                    German   Danish

This, however, is not the whole story. If we go a stage further and compare this Teutonic group with non-Teutonic languages, we discover equally remarkable resemblances. Taking some of the words used before, let us compare their forms in English, representing a Teutonic language, with those found in Latin or Greek, which belong to two different families, the Italic and the Hellenic respectively. We might also include French, which is a modern development from Latin, just as Modern English is from Old English.

English	Latin	French	Greek
one	unus	un	cf. oinos (οἶνος) = *one* (on dice)
two	duo	deux	duo (δύο)
three	tres	trois	treis (τρεῖς)
father	pater	père	pater (πατήρ)
mother	mater	mère	meter (μήτηρ)
brother	frater	frère	phrater (φράτηρ)

The resemblances are not so close as before, but they are too great to be merely accidental. A similar comparison with other languages, such as the Celtic group, would reveal more features in common. As a result of this evidence we can now draw up a more complete table to show the relationship between these larger linguistic units, the Teutonic, Italic, Hellenic, Celtic and other groups. There are altogether nine of these,[4] and they include most of the European and some of the Indian languages. For this reason they are often called the Indo-European family of languages. Another term is the Aryan family. Aryan is thus not a racial but a linguistic label. The people who speak the Aryan or Indo-European languages are not a racial unit; they include, and no doubt always included, many varied stocks. It is difficult to say when or where the parent language from which these groups are descended— primitive Aryan or Indo-European—was originally spoken, except that it was some time before 2000 B.C., possibly 3000 or 4000 B.C. Scholars formerly thought that the original home of this ancestral tongue was somewhere in Asia, but the modern view is that it was more probably in Northern or Central Europe.

[4] Or eleven, if we include the results of recent discoveries.

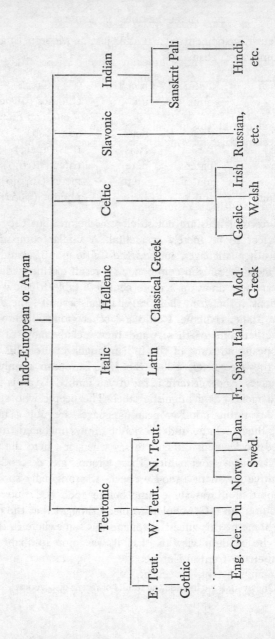

The accompanying diagram shows the relationship of English to the Indo-European family. Again, only the more important languages and groups have been included —the table is considerably reduced and simplified; only six of the nine (or eleven) branches are shown.

A glance at this genealogical table will show that the nearest relatives of English are German and Dutch; the Scandinavian languages are also very close, in some respects actually closer. Rather more distant are Greek and Latin (with its modern descendants French, Spanish and Italian) and the Celtic languages, including the language of the ancient Britons, and modern Celtic forms of speech, such as the Gaelic still spoken in the Highlands of Scotland and in parts of Canada, especially Nova Scotia, the recently revived Irish language of Eire, and the Cymric of Wales.

Outside the Indo-European family and, as far as we know, quite unrelated to it, are many other groups of languages, for instance, the Semitic group to which Hebrew and Arabic belong, another group which includes Chinese, and several besides these. Although they have attained a dominating position because of the political power and prestige of the nations who use them, the Indo-European languages thus constitute only a fraction of the world's total linguistic resources. They may not always maintain that supremacy.

Before leaving this part of the subject it should perhaps be explained that, even if we succeed in tracing languages back to the Indo-European parent-tongue and in reconstructing this primitive form of speech, we are nowhere near the stage at which language actually originated. Primitive Indo-European was a highly developed and complex instrument; for long ages before its appearance man or sub-man must have been articulate. The development of speech is perhaps the most important advance in the history of mankind. There has been much speculation as to how this means of communication was evolved. It is a mystery that may never be solved, as we have so little evidence to guide us. But several theories have been proposed, generally referred to rather disrespectfully by various nicknames. First, there is the "bow-wow" theory, which, as its name suggests, supposes that words were first made from the noises associated with natural objects: the bark of a dog, the noise of the wind, and similar sounds actually became the names of the dog and the wind. This theory has obvious weaknesses; it would at best account for only a limited number of words, as many objects do not make characteristic noises. Then there is the "ding-dong" theory, according to which man reacted to the presence of various external phenomena by making specific noises, just as a bell makes its "ding-dong" under the impact of an outside force. A somewhat similar explanation has been labelled the "pooh-pooh" theory; this attempts to explain words as originally spontaneous exclamations like our modern *Oh!*, *Ouch!*, etc. A more systematic attempt to explain the origin of language has been made by Jespersen,[5] who comes to the conclusion, based on three different lines of enquiry, that language originated in the emotional, song-like outpourings of primitive man, which were gradually canalized into speech. This may be called the "hey nonny nonny!" theory. A later theory has been suggested by Paget.[6] According to this, speech started not as sound but as gestures made by the hands. Then, after a considerable time, when man, in the course of his evolution, had to work so continuously with his hands that they could no longer be used for gesticulating, he carried out the same movements with his tongue inside his mouth; this series of tongue positions, acting on the air which is being inhaled and

[5] Jespersen, *Language: Its Nature, Development and Origin*.
[6] Sir Richard Paget, *Human Speech*.

exhaled, would naturally give rise to definite sounds, which would then replace the original gesture and convey the same meaning. This theory is interesting but not quite convincing. It is obvious that all these explanations are highly speculative; possibly there is no need to assume any *one* way in which language originated; it may have been due to a combination of some of these processes, and perhaps others that have not yet been considered.[7]

[7] Another stimulating discussion of this problem is R. A. Wilson's *The Birth of Language*.

4. The Old English Vocabulary

The vocabulary in Old English times was much smaller than it is today, containing only a small fraction of our modern total of words. It was also much more homogeneous, consisting almost entirely of words of Teutonic origin. But even in these early days the habit of borrowing words from outside sources, which has been so characteristic of English, had already started, though on a very small scale. Of the many thousands of words in O.E. probably less than five hundred were non-Teutonic, about half a dozen Celtic words taken over from the conquered Britons, a few hundred Latin words borrowed at different periods, and, in late O.E., a small number of Scandinavian and French words. For the more wide-spread influence of these last two languages we have to wait till the M.E. period, and it will be convenient to discuss these two important groups of loan-words when we are building up our picture of Middle English.[1]

CELTIC LOAN-WORDS

It was at one time thought that a great many Celtic words had been adopted by the Anglo-Saxons from the language of the subjugated Britons; in fact the easiest way to dispose of any English word whose origin was obscure was to say that it was "Celtic". Gradually, however, the number of these alleged Celtic words was reduced, and now the Celtic element in the O.E. vocabulary is con-

[1] See Ch. 6.

sidered to be almost microscopic. The reason for this was probably that the Britons were largely expelled from central England and took refuge in the extreme West—Wales, Cornwall, etc.—and so did not mingle to any great extent with the invaders and affect their speech.[2] The situation was quite different from that which arose after the Norman Conquest, when victor and vanquished settled down together, and ultimately the conquerors adopted the speech of the conquered.[3] The few words that seem to be of Celtic origin are insignificant: *brocc* (a badger—still heard in dialect) *dunn* (dark-coloured), *dry* (magician—connected with *druid*) and two or three more. But in one direction the ancient Celtic speech had a much greater influence—that is, in English place-names. Many of the larger towns, rivers and mountains retained their early Brito-Celtic names, though these were often modified by the newcomers. We have an exact parallel in North America, where the invading French and English settlers took over many of the earlier Indian geographical names which form so picturesque a feature in our topography—Mississippi, Oswego, Chicago, Kalamazoo, Michigan, Ontario, Ottawa, Saskatchewan, Manitoba, etc. In the same way the Anglo-Saxons preserved old Celtic names of towns such as London, Dover, Manchester, Dorchester (in the last two adding an O.E. ending *ceaster* to a Celtic first element), rivers such as Thames, Avon, Dee, Severn, Ouse, and mountains like the Pennines, Helvellyn.

LATIN LOAN-WORDS

The Latin borrowings constitute by far the greatest non-Teutonic element in the O.E. vocabulary. They can

---

[2] There is, however, some disagreement among historians about this question.

[3] See p. 77.

be divided into several groups according to the period
when they entered the language.

(1) Continental Borrowings

Even before the Teutonic tribes crossed over the sea to
England they had been in contact with soldiers and colonists from Rome, whose language had already provided
them with a number of words. These can generally be
recognized because of certain sounds they contain and because they are common in Continental Teutonic languages. One of the greatest achievements of the Romans
in the regions they conquered consisted in the building of
good roads, in place of the primitive tracks and footpaths
that had previously existed. To these roads they gave the
Latin term *strata via*, 'paved road'. After a time the word
via was dropped and the term *strata*, borrowed by the
English while they were still on the Continent, reached
England in the form *strǣt*, which has given us our modern *street*. The same Latin word shows itself in a slightly
different form in the German *strasse*, the Swedish *stråt*
and the Danish *strǣde*. As it is thus a common Teutonic
loan-word it seems to go back to this early continental
period of the language. Other terms of a military nature
were introduced during the same period: *weall* (wall)
from Latin *vallum* (rampart), *mīl* (mile) from *mille pas-
sus* (1000 paces). Some commercial terms were also
brought over: *mynet* (coin—cf. Mod. *mint*) from Latin
moneta, *pund* (pound), Lat. *pondus* (weight), *ynce*
(inch), Lat. *unoia* (cf. ounce). Many names of articles of
food were borrowed; a few are *wīn* (wine), Lat. *vinum*,
cīese (cheese), Lat. *caseus*, *butere* (butter), Lat. *butyrum*.
Two religious terms may be noted: *cirice* (church) from
Greek *kuriakon* (κυριακόν)[4] and *biscop* (bishop) from

---

[4] This seems to be a direct loan from Greek, not, like many

46

Lat. *episcopus*. For all these words similar terms can be found in Continental Teutonic languages. Finally, we may mention the exceptional word *Sæternesdæg* (Saturday), the one day that is named in honour of a Roman god, Saturn, in striking contrast to the rest of the days of the week, which enshrine Teutonic words: the sun, the moon, the Northern gods Tiw, Woden, Thor and the goddess Frig. These Teutonic deities are substitutes for the Roman Mars, Mercury, Jove and Venus, whose names can be seen in the French terms for the days of the week.

(2) *Latin Words Borrowed in England*

These later loan-words come from two sources:

(a) Words which the Britons had adopted during the Roman occupation of the country (43–410) and which were later taken over by the Anglo-Saxons.

(b) Words introduced into England by the Roman missionaries and in other ways after the gradual conversion of the country to Christianity, from 597 onwards.

The first group is very small; the most important word is O.E. *ceaster* from Lat. *castra* (camp), which appears in various forms in many place-names, e.g. Chester, Leicester, Dorchester, Lancaster. Another is Lat. *portus* (harbour), which gives English *port*; this word is seen in the name Portsmouth.

The second group is far more numerous and constitutes the most important contribution of Latin to the O.E. vocabulary. It consists mainly of religious terms, many of which are found in Mod. E. We cannot always state with absolute certainty whether some of these words were borrowed at this time or in the Continental period. The fol-

---

other Greek words, introduced through Latin. The Latin word for church, *ecclesia*, is seen in the word *ecclesiastical*, the Fr. *église*, Welsh *eglwys*.

lowing are a few examples, the modern forms of the words being given; as a rule the O.E. forms are very similar: *abbot*, *abbess*, *angel*, *candle*, *disciple*, *martyr*, *mass*, *monk*, *nun*, *organ*, *pope*, *priest*, *psalm*, *school*, *temple*. In addition a number of botanical names are taken over, including *lily*, *pear*, *pine*, *box*, and miscellaneous terms such as *dish*, *fork*, *chalk*, *cook*, *cup*, etc.

There are several hundred words in this group.

Sometimes, instead of borrowing new terms, there is an attempt to translate the idea behind the Latin word into English, a process common in German. Thus the word *trinitas* is reproduced in O.E. as *ðrīnes* (=threeness), *evangelium* as *gōdspell* (=the good story or message, Mod. *gospel*), *misericordia* as *mildheortedness*. A few of these words, such as *gospel*, have survived, but most have been lost. Sometimes a word that originally denoted a pagan idea was adapted to the purposes of Christianity; thus O.E. *blēdsian*, which originally meant to consecrate with blood while sacrificing, takes on a new Christian connotation and gives us our word *bless*.

These borrowings in O.E. must be viewed against a background of the total vocabulary. They are to a considerable extent technical in character and do not enter into our everyday life so deeply and intimately as the vast Teutonic residue. But they are important historically and socially, because in all ages the words that are borrowed by one language from another reflect the kind of cultural contact that existed between two peoples, one providing the new word, the other adopting it. A study of these words will show how, at the very outset of our history, in such important departments of life as religion, warfare and commerce, Roman influence has coloured our speech and provided the first significant contribution to the variegated pattern of our abundant modern vocabulary.

The native Teutonic portion of the O.E. vocabulary is

much more varied. It contains most of the basic words in our modern speech; the language of works such as the Bible, *Pilgrim's Progress*, and the popular ballads shows a very large proportion of words derived from this source. They are the words we use in our everyday conversation, the words denoting the home and its various parts, *house, home, roof, door, ground*, etc., terms for human beings and animals, *man, woman, child, horse, cow, sheep, ox*, the intimate family relationships, *father, mother, brother, son, daughter*—the more remote relationships are, as we shall see, indicated by words of French origin[5]—parts of the body, *hand, arm, head, foot, nose, ear, eye*—but not *face*—abstract conceptions such as *life, death, God, heaven, hell; dark, light; good, evil; glad, sorry; love, hate; much, little; young, old*, the constituents of the universe, *world, earth, sun, moon, stars*, the divisions of time, *night, day, noon, evening*, and innumerable other equally essential words. It must not be thought, however, that O.E. was restricted to words of this primitive type. The language also had a very elaborate poetical vocabulary, much of which has disappeared. Its ornate character suggests a long poetic tradition. One of its most striking features was the use of the *kenning*, a poetical device by which an object was described in an indirect manner, often by a striking metaphor. Thus the sea is the "whalepath" or the "swan's road", the boat the "wave-courser", the sword the "leavings of the hammers". There is a rich variety of these poetical synonyms; in *Beowulf* we can find about forty terms for the ocean, about thirty for a hall or a house, about twenty for a sword or for a man. Most of these, as well as a great many other terms in the O.E. vocabulary, have not survived. One feels that the language is sometimes the poorer because of this. Take, for instance, two words which existed in O.E.: *woruldhād* and *munuchād*, literally,

5 See p. 80.

"worldhood" and "monkhood". To convey the ideas behind these words today we have to say *secular life* and *monastic life*. There are two drawbacks to the modern as opposed to the O.E. terms. First we have to use two words instead of one to express our meaning. This is not of great importance; but a more serious disadvantage is that we have to bring in a word *secular*, which to many people is not immediately intelligible; *worldhood*, if it had survived, would be a "democratic" word. This point has already been discussed in Chapter 2.

A large number of words were also replaced later by French words, e.g. O.E. *ēam*, for which *uncle* was substituted in M.E., O.E. *fierd*, *here*, displaced by *army*. This process is discussed in detail in Chapter 6.

So as to provide a concrete illustration of this stage of the language, three short passages are appended, with a literal translation of extracts 2 and 3. First the O.E. version of the Lord's Prayer is given; it will be noted that the amount of difference between this and the modern version is not so great as in the other pieces; the reason is, of course, that so many of the words used in this utterance have remained in the language. Secondly, a short passage from the story of Caedmon as told by Bede in Latin and translated into O.E., possibly by King Alfred, and, finally, a more difficult extract, the opening of the epic poem *Beowulf*, the most important literary work of the period.

Fæder ure, þu þe eart on heofonum, si þin nama gehalgod. Tobecume þin rice. Gewurþe ðin willa on eorðan swa swa on heofonum. Urne gedæghwamlican hlaf syle us to dæg. And forgyf us ure gyltas, swa swa we forgyfað urum gyltendum. And ne gelæd þu us on costnunge, ac alys us of yfele. Soþlice.

Wæs he se mon in weoruldhade geseted oð þa
Was he the man in worldhood established until the
tide þe he wæs gelyfdre ylde, ond næfre nænig leoð
time that he was of advanced age, and never no song
geleornade. Ond he for þon oft in gebeorscipe,
[had] learned. And he for this often at a banquet
þonne þær wæs blisse intinga gedemed,
when there [it] was for the sake of mirth decided
þæt heo ealle sceolden þurh endebyrdnesse be
that they all should in order to the
hearpan singan, þonne he geseah þa hearpan him
harp sing, when he saw the harp him
nealecan, þonne aras he for scome from þæm
approach, then arose he for shame from that
symble, ond ham eode to his huse.
feast, and home went to his house.

Hwæt, we Gar-dena in geardagum
Lo! we of the Spear-Danes in former days

Þeodcyninga þrym gefrunon,
Of the kings of the people the glory heard,

Hu ða æþelingas ellen fremedon!
How the heroes valour performed.

Oft Scyld Scefing sceaþena þreatum,
Often Scyld, son of Sceaf, from the enemies' troops

Monegum mægþum meodosetla ofteah,
[From] many tribes [their] mead-benches took away,

Egsode eorlas, syððan ærest wearð
Terrified the warriors, since first [he] was

Feasceaft funden.
Abandoned found.

51

5. The Structure of Old English

When the Angles and Saxons and other Teutonic tribes settled in England, they did not speak a uniform language but a group of closely related dialects. As a result there was considerable variety in the speech of the different regions in which these peoples lived. This diversity is still reflected to some extent in our modern dialects. The speech of the farmer or miner of Northumberland, the shepherd of the Sussex downs, and the village store-keeper of Vermont, the fisherman of Nova Scotia may have its roots in the ancient language of 1500 years ago. At the period of settlement the Angles, the Saxons, and the Jutes at first established separate kingdoms, which are shown on the map (p. 36). We still find traces of this division in such names as East Anglia, Sussex (the South Saxons), Essex (the East Saxons), Wessex (the West Saxons). In modern times the term Wessex has been revived by Thomas Hardy to indicate the background of his "Wessex" novels.

Four main dialects of Old English are generally distinguished; see map, p. 53.

(1) Northumbrian, spoken, as its name indicates, north of the River Humber in Yorkshire and extending to the Rivers Forth and Clyde in Scotland, thus including the southern part of Scotland, which from a linguistic point of view is to be linked with the northern half of England.

(2) Mercian, between the Humber and the Thames, i.e. the central portion of England.

(3) West Saxon, between the Thames and the English Channel.

(4) Kentish, in the extreme south-east.

In the south-west (Cornwall) a Celtic form of speech survived; in Wales a Celtic tongue can still be heard today.

In early O.E. the Northumbrian dialect was the most important because the chief centres of culture were in the north, monasteries like Jarrow and Whitby, where scholars such as the Venerable Bede bore aloft the torch of religion and culture. Later, however, owing to changed political conditions and the ravages of the Vikings in the north and east of England during the ninth and tenth centuries, English culture was largely transferred to Wessex, especially during the reign of King Alfred (d. 901). As a result the West Saxon dialect replaced Northumbrian as the dominant form of the language. Most of our Old English literature has come down to us in this dialect. Some of it was no doubt originally written in the Northumbrian dialect, but it has been transcribed into West Saxon in the versions that have survived. The account of Old English given here will therefore be based on West Saxon. In M.E., as we shall see, a further shift in the relative importance of the dialects takes place; Mercian then replaces West Saxon as the leading dialect, and so becomes the ancestor of our "standard" modern English speech.

THE LEADING FEATURES OF OLD ENGLISH

It will be convenient to examine O.E. under the separate headings of sounds, forms, vocabulary and syntax. Only a brief discussion of each can be given, mainly to show the contrast with Mod. E.

The Sounds of O.E.

(1) CONSONANTS

The O.E. consonant system shows many differences from that of Mod. E. First, there were no silent consonants; words such as *cnāwan, cnēo* (know, knee) were pronounced with the sounds *k+n, gnāwan* (gnaw), *gnornian* (lament), with *g+n, wrītan* (to write) with *w+r*, etc. It is a useful vocal exercise to try to articulate these sounds. These double consonants were not reduced to single sounds till quite late in the history of English.

O.E. had several consonants that we do not find in Mod. E. The letter *h* had two sounds which have been completely lost. It might be pronounced like our modern *h*, e.g. as in *hit* (Mod. E. *it*), *hearpe* (harp). But in words like *riht, niht* (right, night) it had the sound we hear in German *ich, Reich*. The same sound can still be heard in the Scottish dialectal pronunciation of these words (*recht, nicht*). In words like *sōhte* (sought) the *h* had the sound heard in Scottish *loch* or German *doch*. The silent *gh* in our modern spelling is a reflection of these two vanished sounds.

Other letters in O.E. had a double pronunciation according to the sounds that followed or preceded them. Thus in late O.E. *g* was pronounced like *g* in *go* in words like *gān* (to go), *gold, guma* (man), but in words like *gēar* (year), *gieldan* (yield), *gif* (if) it had the sound of *y* in *yet*. The letter *c* also had a twofold value; in words like *can, corn, cūðe* (could) it had a *k*-sound, in *cild* (child), *cealc* (chalk), *cirice* (church) approximately the sound of *ch*.

The two sounds of *th* (as in *thin* and *then*) were indicated in O.E. by two symbols which have since disappeared, ð and þ. These were not used consistently to denote these two different sounds, i.e. the symbol ð might sometimes stand for the *th* sound in *thin*, sometimes the sound in *then*; the same is true of þ. In M.E. ð and þ were replaced by *th*, but before this happened þ had sometimes been confused with *y*. This explains our mock-antique modern form *ye* as in *Ye olde hatte shoppe*, where the *ye* is really a form of *the*, earlier *þe*.

O.E. also had a special symbol for the sound of *w*, but this is not usually reproduced in O.E. texts.

The letters *f*, *s* and ð (or þ) had two pronunciations according to their position in the O.E. word, a phenomenon that is still reflected to some extent in Mod. E. At the beginning or the end of a word they had the sounds of *f*, *s*, and the *th* in *thin*, often called "breathed" sounds. In the middle of a word, especially between vowels, they had the corresponding "voiced" sounds, *v*, *z*, and the *th* in *then*. This accounts for pairs of words in Mod. E. like *loaf, loaves, knife, knives, bath, bathe*. In the O.E. word for *loaf* (*hlāf*) the *f* was final and so had the usual sound of *f*; in the plural *hlāfas* it was medial and therefore had a *v*-sound, which is shown in the modern *loaves*. This is one of the few cases where our modern spelling is better than O.E. or M.E. spelling. Similarly we have *sittan, ðus* (sit, thus) with an *s*-sound at the beginning and the end of the words but *frēosan* (freeze) with the sound *z* medially. This *z*-sound is not always shown in the modern spelling; thus *rise* (O.E. *rīsan*) has the same sound as *freeze* for the same reason, but *s* is kept in the spelling. The noun *bath* goes back to O.E. *bæð* with a final ð, while the verb *bathe* is from *baðian* with a medial ð which has a different sound. Here again no difference is made in the modern spelling, though the pronunciation of the *th* differs in the two words. The pronunciation in Mod. E. does not, however, always agree with that found in O.E.; in a large group of words, for instance, ð has become "voiced" initially in

Mod. E., e.g. *the, this, that, these, them, than, then*. In O.E., according to the rule stated above, ð was "breathed" in this group.

(2) VOWELS

One vowel *symbol* is seen in O.E. which we do not have in Mod. E. This is *æ*, used to denote a sound similar to that of *a* in the word *cat*. O.E. also had a vowel *sound* which does not exist in Mod. E. but which is found in French and German. This sound was written *y* and was approximately the same as the vowel in French *lune* or *rue* or German *müde*. Like *æ* and the other O.E. vowels, it might be either long or short. The other vowel sounds are not unlike those of Mod. E., though they do not occur in the same words. We have always to allow for changes during the long history of English, and a word which has a certain vowel sound in O.E. is very likely to appear in Mod. E. with quite a different one. Generally speaking, the short vowels of O.E. are more stable than the long ones; they often remain unchanged right down into Mod. E., while the long vowels and diphthongs change very greatly. Thus O.E. *ā*, the sound in *father*, has become "long o" in Mod. E. (*stān* > stone, etc.). O.E. *ū*, the sound in *moon*, has become *ou* or *ow* (*cū, hūs* > cow, house, etc.).

The following table gives the vowels of O.E. with examples of words in which they occur and their normal equivalents in Mod. E.

O.E. Vowel[1]	O.E. Words	Mod. E. Words
ā	hām, bān, āc, stān	home, bone, oak, stone
a	man(n), lamb	man, lamb
ǣ	dǣd, sǣd	deed, seed
æ	æt, glæd	at, glad
ē	wē, fēt	we, feet
e	settan, wel	set, well
ī	mīn, tīd	mine, tide
i	sittan, hit	sit, it
ō	gōd, sōna	good, soon
o	God, cocc	God, cock
ū	hūs, ūt, cū, mūs	house, out, cow, mouse
u	ful, lufu	full, love
ȳ	hȳdan, mȳs	hide, mice
y	pytt, synn	pit, sin

In studying this table note that the vowels in the O.E. words are pronounced approximately as follows: ā has the sound of *a* in *father*, *a* the same sound short or about the vowel in German *Man*, ē has the sound in *name*, ī has the sound in *see*, ō the sound in *go*, ū the sound in *too*, and ȳ has the French or German sounds described above (*lune*, etc.) The remaining O.E. vowels, short *e*, *i*, *o*, *u*, are pronounced about as in Mod. E. *well*, *it*, *God*, *full*.

Note that O.E. ȳ and *y* give the same result in Mod. E. as O.E. ī and *i*, that ǣ and ē produce the same sound in Mod. E., as do also *a* and *æ*.

It must also be emphasized that the developments and equivalents shown above are frequently disturbed by other factors, so that there are many exceptions to the rules suggested here. Some of these will be discussed and explained later.

[1] The O.E. manuscripts very seldom indicate any difference between long and short vowels. The mark denoting length (ā, etc.) is a modern convenience. It is used in this book for isolated words; in longer phrases the O.E. practice is followed.

In addition to these simple vowels O.E., like Mod. E., had a number of diphthongs. By a diphthong is meant a combination of two vowels which form one syllable, as in Mod. E. *boil, town.* Examples of O.E. diphthongs are *ēo* as in O.E. *dēop,* Mod. E. *deep, eo* as in O.E. *eorðe,* Mod. E. *earth, ēa* as in O.E. *lēaf,* Mod. E. *leaf, ea* as in O.E. *weall,* Mod. E. *wall.*

The Forms of O.E.

No complete account can be given in a short space of the forms or morphology of O.E. Only some of the outstanding features can be indicated, and, as usual, they will be chosen so as to show the relations between O.E. and Mod. E.

The Noun

The O.E. noun had grammatical and not logical gender.[2] Thus *stān* 'stone' is masculine, *lār,* 'lore, teaching' feminine, and *gēar, hors, wīf* 'year, horse, woman' are neuter. The forms or declension of the noun varied in these three classes. Other features besides gender affected the pattern of the noun, and we find in O.E. about twenty different types. But many of these include only a small number of nouns, and very few have left any traces in Mod. E. or even in M.E. We shall mention here only those that are reflected in the modern language.

TYPE 1: HUND 'DOG' (MASCULINE)

This declension has provided the pattern for most of our modern nouns, i.e. with a plural and possessive in *s* or *es* (*dog, dogs; fish, fishes*). The complete O.E. declen-

[2] For the explanation of these terms see p. 25.

sion is given here, with the Mod. E. forms that have
survived.

	Singular	Plural
Nominative	hund (hound)	hundas (hounds)
Accusative	" "	" "
Genitive	hundes (hound's)	hunda
Dative	hunde	hundum

Of the six forms present in O.E. three have completely
disappeared: *hunde, hunda, hundum*. One word still
shows a trace of the dative plural ending –*um*; this can be
seen in the archaic *whilom*, in which the –*om* is a relic
of O.E. –*um*, the form in O.E. being *hwīlum*, meaning
'at times', from *hwīl*, 'time'.

TYPE 2: SCĒAP 'SHEEP' (NEUTER)

This is identical with Type 1 except that the Nom. and
Acc. plural has no –*as* ending, i.e. it has the same form as
the Nom. and Acc. singular. There are still traces of this
declension in Mod. E.; we may call it "the unchanged
plural declension". Many names of animals belong to this
type in O.E. *Sheep, deer* and *swine* still follow it; they
were *scēap, dēor* and *swīn* in both singular and plural in
O.E. But *horse*, which also belonged here in O.E., has
gone over to Type 1 in Mod. E. O.E. *gēar* (year) still
shows this unchanged plural in such phrases as "a two-
year-old".

TYPE 3: OXA 'OX' (MASCULINE)—ALSO INCLUDES FEMININE AND NEUTER NOUNS

This type presents quite a different pattern; the characteristic ending is –*an*, found in five out of the eight
forms.

	Singular	*Plural*
Nominative	oxa (ox)	oxan (oxen)
Accusative	oxan	"
Genitive	"	oxena
Dative	"	oxum

Of the many nouns in this declension in O.E. only one shows any trace of it in Mod. E.—*ox, oxen.* The plurals *children, brethren, kine,* which look as if they belong to this type, developed the –*n* forms later by analogy; they belonged to quite different declensions in O.E. The genitive in this class had no *s*; traces of this *s*-less possessive will be found later on in M.E., and we still have a "fossil" form in the expression *Lady Day,* normally *Lady's Day* or *the Day of Our Lady*; this has no –*s* because in O.E. its genitive was formed in –*an* (*hlǣfdīgan dæg*).

TYPE 4: GŌS 'GOOSE' (FEMININE)—ALSO INCLUDES MASCU-
LINE NOUNS

This shows a completely different kind of inflection. Instead of forming the nominative and accusative plural by an ending as in Types 1 and 3, this class of noun changes the root-vowel; thus *gōs* becomes *gēs*, *fōt* becomes *fēt*, etc.[3] The same change is seen in the dative singular. This is still reflected in a group of Mod. nouns: *foot, feet; tooth, teeth; mouse, mice; man, men,* etc. The O.E. declension is as follows:

---

[3] This is one example of a very wide-spread process in O.E. and other Teutonic languages. It is known as *i*-umlaut or *i*-mutation. Cf. German *mann*, plural *männer* (*ä* = short *e*), Swedish *man*, plural *män*, etc. It occurs in other parts of speech as well, e.g. *old, elder, eldest.*

	Singular	*Plural*
Nominative	gōs (goose)	gēs (geese)
Accusative	"	"
Genitive	gōse or gēs	gōsa
Dative	gēs	gōsum

O.E. had more nouns of this type than Mod. E. As in the case of Type 3, many have gone over to the dominant Type 1 with a plural in s. Thus bōc (book) had a plural bēc; this should have given Mod. E. book, plural beek (or possibly beech), just like foot, feet. But the influence of the great number of plurals in s was too strong, and so by analogy we get books. In this declension nouns in ō changed this to ē, those with ū changed to ȳ (e.g. mūs, plural mȳs; Mod. mouse, mice), a (o) changed to e (man(n) or mon(n), plural men(n)). As we have no special form for the dative case in Mod. E., the vowel change in this form cannot show itself, but there is one interesting trace of it in place-names. The word burg 'fortified place, town' belonged to this declension and had a dative byrg. This is reflected in the ending –bury, as in Canterbury from O.E. [æt] Cantwara byrg, 'at the town of the people of Kent', æt taking the dative. But the nominative or accusative burg or burh is seen in the word borough and in the endings of place-names such as Edinburgh or Peterborough.

The Adjective

Because it is such a striking example of the reduction of forms in English the two types of declension of the adjective gōd (good) are given in full. The "weak" declension is found in a phrase like sē gōda man 'the good man', the "strong" declension in ān gōd man 'a good man' or *gōd wīn* 'good wine'. The adjective in Mod. German has a similar double declension.

WEAK
Singular

	Masculine	Feminine	Neuter
Nom.	gōda	gōde	gōde
Acc.	gōdan	gōdan	gōde
Gen.	"	"	gōdan
Dat.	"	"	"

Plural (all genders)

Nom., Acc.	gōdan
Gen.	gōdena or gōdra
Dat.	gōdum

STRONG
Singular

	Masculine	Feminine	Neuter
Nom.	gōd	gōd	gōd
Acc.	gōdne	gōde	gōd
Gen.	gōdes	gōdre	gōdes
Dat.	gōdum	"	gōdum

Plural

	Masculine	Feminine	Neuter
Nom., Acc.	gōde	gōda; -e	gōd(e)
Gen.	gōdra	gōdra	gōdra
Dat.	gōdum	gōdum	gōdum

This whole system has completely disappeared in Mod. E. In M.E., as we shall see, a single inflection –*e*– was left.[4]

The Definite Article (=Mod. E. *the*)

Here, too, we have a good illustration of simplification in M.E. and O.E. These are the most usual forms of the article in O.E.

[4] See Ch. 7.

	Singular			*Plural*
	Masculine	Feminine	Neuter	(all genders)
Nom.	sē	sēo	ðæt	ðā
Acc.	ðone	ðā	"	"
Gen.	ðæs	ðǣre	ðæs	ðāra
Dat.	ðǣm	"	ðǣm	ðǣm

It will be noted that some of these forms have survived in Mod. E. as pronouns, e.g. ðæt > that. But *the* in Mod. E. is invariable; it has arisen through the substitution of the ð sound, found in almost all the forms, for the s of sē.

The Verb

As in Mod. E., there are two classes of verbs in O.E., strong and weak.[5] Examples in Mod. E. are:

(1) *Strong*   ride   rode   ridden
                   sing   sang   sung
(2) *Weak*   hope   hoped   hoped
                   keep   kept   kept

It will be seen that while strong verbs usually form the past tense and past participle by changing the root vowel, weak verbs add –*ed* or –*t*; the root vowel may change, but this is not essential.

STRONG VERBS

In O.E. we can distinguish seven classes of strong verbs. The principal parts of Class I and Class III are given as illustrations, as these two classes are well represented in Mod. E.

---

[5] The terms *old* and *new*, sometimes used for these two classes, are misleading, as both categories seem to be equally old. They have their roots far back in Primitive Teutonic.

Class I

Infinitive	Past Sing.	Past Plural
rīdan (to ride)	rād (rode)	ridon
wrītan (to write)	wrāt (wrote)	writon

Past Participle

(ge)riden (ridden)
(ge)writen (written)

Note that in O.E. there are two forms of the past tense; in Mod. E. only one, usually descended from the past singular. Occasionally, however, the past plural has given our modern form, e.g. *bite*, *bit*; if this verb had followed the normal pattern shown above we should say *I bite* (present) and *I bote* (past), with the same pattern as *write*, *wrote*.

Class III

Infinitive	Past Sing.	Past Plural
singan (to sing)	sang (sang)	sungon
drincan (to drink)	dranc (drank)	druncon

Past Participle

(ge)sungen (sung)
(ge)druncen (drunk)

Class III has several other varieties, but this is the most common and is well represented in Mod. E. Here, as in Class I, the two forms of the past have been reduced to one.

It will be observed that in all uncompounded O.E. verbs, both weak and strong, a prefix *ge-* might be found in the past participle. This, as we shall see, becomes *y-* in M.E. and disappears in Mod. E., except in a few archaisms like *yclept*.

The remaining five classes of O.E. strong verbs do not, as a rule, develop so regularly in Mod. E.

WEAK VERBS

The main types of O.E. weak verbs are illustrated by the following examples.

Infinitive	Past Sing.	Past Plural
hīeran (to hear)	hīerde (heard)	hīerdon
sēcan (to seek)	sōhte (sought)	sōhton
leornian (to learn)	leornode (learned)	leornodon

Past Participle

(ge)hīered (heard)
(ge)sōht (sought)
(ge)leornod (learned)

Unlike the strong verbs, these verbs show no difference in the vowel of the past singular and plural. The general resemblance of this type to Mod. E. is obvious.

Besides these fairly regular types of O.E. verbs there are many, as in Mod. E., which show a quite irregular pattern, e.g. *gān* (to go), *bēon* or *wesan* (to be).

On this foundation of the principal parts of the verb is built the complete conjugation. Some of its forms, such as the endings of the present tense in *–est*, *–eð*, still persist in archaic Mod. E.; others such as the *–on* seen above in the past plural, have vanished. One striking difference is in the ending of the present participle, which in O.E. was *–ende* (*singende, hīerende*, etc.) but in Mod. E. has been replaced by the ending *–ing* (*singing, hearing*).

Pronouns

Many forms of the O.E. pronouns are no longer used. Some have dropped out altogether, others have been changed. If we look at the third personal pronoun (*he, she, it*) its pattern will be seen to resemble that of the definite article, but many more forms have survived.

Singular

	Masculine	Feminine	Neuter
Nom.	hē (he)	hēo (she?)	hit (it)
Acc.	hine	hie	"
Gen.	his (his)	hire (her)	his
Dat.	him (him)	"	him

Plural (all genders)

Nom.	hie
Acc.	"
Gen.	hira or heora
Dat.	him or heom

The Acc. *hine* has been lost; modern *him* is, as we see, originally the dative. It is doubtful whether *she* is descended from *hēo*.[6] Note that we have a new neuter genitive pronoun, *its*, in Mod. E.; till the seventeenth century *his* was still used where today we use *its*; this can be observed in the Authorized Version of the Bible (1611).

The other pronouns show somewhat similar developments. One of the most striking changes, in which Mod. E. differs radically from O.E., and indeed from most other languages, is the levelling of the singular and plural pronouns of the second person. In O.E. these were:

	Singular	Plural
Nom.	ðū (thou)	gē (ye)
Acc.	ðē (thee)	ēow (you)

In archaic Mod. E. this difference is still shown, but today we use the one form *you* for both singular and plural, nominative and accusative, except in biblical and

[6] See p. 76.

poetical language and the speech of Quakers, who use *thee*. This reduction of four pronouns to one might be added to the examples given in Chapter 2 to illustrate the simplification of Mod. E. forms.

Adverbs

There were several methods in O.E. of forming adverbs from adjectives; in Mod. E. the process usually consists of the addition of *–ly*, e.g. *glad, gladly*. This is a common method in O.E. too; the corresponding ending was *–līce*, giving us O.E. *glæd, glædlīce*. But there were two other ways that are of importance because they have left traces in Mod. E. One was to add *–e* instead of *–līce* to the adjective, e.g. *fæst, fæste*. This final *e* was lost in the early modern period, and consequently today there is no difference in form between the adjective and the adverb in this type of O.E. adverb. We can say *a fast train* (adj.) or *the train went fast* (adv.). This explains the adverbial use of *slow*, where, however, a new adverb *slowly* has arisen by analogy. A third type of O.E. adverb was seen in certain nouns which could be used adverbially in the genitive case. A modern relic of this is found in such North American idioms as *he works nights*, where *nights* is not historically a plural but a genitive singular (*nihtes*) used as an adverb (=*by night*).

SYNTAX

It is difficult to discuss the syntax of a language in any detail unless the reader has a knowledge of the language in question, so that only a few outstanding features of O.E. syntax will be given here.

The arrangement of the words in an O.E. sentence was frequently quite different from Mod. E. There was a tendency, as in Mod. German, to place the verb at the end of the sentence, though this is not so regular as in German. But we find, for instance, such phrases as *se cyning friõ nam*, literally "the king peace made" instead of "made peace" or *him õa aõas sworon*, "to him oaths they swore". Often, however, a sentence will begin with the verb; this is done to secure variety and emphasis and is not altogether unknown in Mod. E. Here is a simple example: *wæs se hungor on õæs cyninges dagum on Egyptum*, "[there] was the famine in the days of that king in Egypt". This device is especially frequent in poetry, e.g. *com õa to recede rinc siõian*, "came then to the hall the warrior march(ing)", which reminds one of the early movie captions: "came the dawn".

The last sentence quoted illustrates another curious syntactical feature in O.E., the use of an infinitive *siõian* (to go) where in Mod. E. we should find a present participle (*going*). Cf. also *se martyr hine geseah standan*, "the martyr saw him standing", literally, "to stand".

A verb of motion is sometimes omitted in O.E., e.g. *hira ne mehte nan to oõrum*, "none of them could [go] to the others"; the word *go* is not expressed in the O.E. phrase *õeos boc sceal to Wiogoraceastre* "this book will [go] to Worcester". This reminds one of similar idioms in modern colloquial and dialect speech, e.g. *I want* [*to go*] *out*. A similar example is *fram ic ne wille*, "I will not [go] away"; this is parallel to phrases like "let's away" in archaic Mod. E.

In many constructions in O.E. we find a genitive or dative form where Mod. E. does not show this feature. Thus the verbs *bidan*, to await, *healdan*, to hold, possess, govern the genitive. We may quote *he õær bad westanwindes*, "he awaited there a west wind" literally "of a west wind". A genitive is often found after a number or a word denoting quantity: *fela godra manna,* "many good men", literally "many *of* good men".

We note the wide-spread use of the subjunctive in O.E., a form of the verb that has almost disappeared today. It is often found in subordinate sentences depending on a main verb such as *to say, to think,* etc., e.g. *he sæde ðæt Norðmanna land wære swyðe lang,* "he said that the land of the Northmen was (lit. were) very long"; *wære* here is the subjunctive as in Mod. E. *if I were;* it could not be used in a modern translation.

The frequent occurrence in O.E. of a repeated negative has already been indicated.[7]

[7] See p. 20.

6. The Middle English Language; the Blending of English and French

Middle English (1100–1500) is a time of rapid change. At the end of the O.E. period, about 1100, we still have a form of English that looks like a foreign tongue; by 1300 the language has taken on an appearance that is much more like modern English, and by the second half of the fourteenth century Chaucer's works no longer present any serious difficulty to the intelligent reader of to-day. The three centuries from 1100 to 1400 saw a far more radical change in our language than the five centuries that have elapsed since. How is this to be explained? The suggestion used to be made that these far-reaching developments between O.E. and M.E. were entirely due to the influence of the Norman Conquest, which introduced French into England, where it was spoken for about three centuries after 1066. This certainly accounts to a great extent for the change in vocabulary, but M.E. shows equally striking modifications in the other departments of the language—sounds, forms and syntax—which cannot all be ascribed to French influence. Even in late O.E. a tendency towards the weakening of some of the endings had already appeared; inflections such as *-on*, *-an*, *-um* were confused; there seems no doubt that this process of slurring and ultimate loss of inflections would have continued even without the impact of a foreign language. But it is certain that the contact, first with the Scandinavian languages in the late O.E. period and, still more, with French during the M.E. period, accelerated this natural tendency towards simplification. When two groups of

NORTHERN

WEST MIDLAND

EAST MIDLAND

R. Humber

R. Thames

SOUTHERN

KENTISH

people or two individuals with different languages have to communicate they tend to concentrate on the essentials of the words they use, and the finer points such as inflections are inevitably neglected. This may perhaps account for the rapidity with which English passed from a highly inflected or synthetic language to one that had little trace of inflection and was largely analytic. On the other hand important factors that help to explain the relatively smaller degree of change after 1500 are, as we have already seen, the invention of printing and the consequent increasing influence of the written language, together with the spread of education, both of which tend to check rapid linguistic development.

MIDDLE ENGLISH DIALECTS

Although the M.E. dialects were descended from those of O.E. there is a change in the names by which they are known and also in their relative importance. The O.E. dialect of Northumbria is now called the Northern dialect, the dialect of Mercia is called Midland, and the dialect of the ancient kingdom of Wessex is now the Southern dialect of M.E. Kentish still retains its old name. The Midland dialect, which extends over the central portion of England, is sub-divided into East Midland and West Midland. (See Map, p. 72.) Gradually, during the M.E. period, the East Midland dialect (E. Midl.) comes to the fore, thus ousting the Southern dialect, the descendant of the Wessex speech which was predominant in later O.E. The E. Midl. dialect is to maintain this position of supremacy permanently; its influence, both on the spoken and the written language, extends far beyond its original geographical limits; the other dialects ultimately become merely local varieties of speech.

There were several reasons for the increasing importance of E. Midl. First, it occupied a favourable geographical position, midway between North and South, communicating with both regions and thus exerting an influence in both directions. It also had within its boundaries the two important cultural centres of Oxford and Cambridge, whose universities were already flourishing in the M.E. period. London, the capital, was just on its border, and the speech of this city was largely E. Midl., though with some traces of the Southern dialect. Secondly, certain outstanding literary works were written in this dialect, the most important being the poems of Chaucer and Wyclif's translation of the Bible; this undoubtedly helped to add to the prestige of this form of speech. Thirdly, it showed a compromise between the extremes of the North and the South; the Northern dialect tended to be somewhat more rapid in its development, the Southern rather slow; E. Midl. changes at a medium pace, steering a middle course between the innovations of the North and the conservatism of the South. Thus its position as a national form of speech is strengthened, and it becomes the ancestor of the most general type of modern English, no longer restricted to any one area but used by people with a certain kind of education and background in any part of the country, a social rather than a regional dialect. This so-called "Standard" English thus has as its basis the E. Midl. regional dialect, though with a slight mixture of forms from the other dialects, especially Southern and Kentish.

THE MIDDLE ENGLISH VOCABULARY

The impact of two other languages, Scandinavian and French, has left far-reaching effects on M.E., mainly in the vocabulary, but also to some extent in sounds, spelling, forms and syntax. Though the English were in contact with these foreign tongues before the beginning of the M.E. period, it is not until M.E. that the effects show themselves on any large scale; they may have influenced popular speech at an earlier date, but the usual lag between this and the language of literature probably accounts for the late appearance of the Scandinavian and French colouring in English. The Viking invaders from Scandinavia, chiefly Danes, attacked England during the ninth and tenth centuries. At the same time as they crossed the Atlantic and carried out the first landing of Europeans on the American continent, these bold and enterprising wanderers had been ravaging the North and East of England, until a large part of the country was in their possession. Like the English, they were largely of Teutonic descent and spoke a language not unlike O.E. (See Table p. 38.) Many of their words were similar, some identical, so that the adoption of Scandinavian terms would present no difficulty; they could easily be fitted into the regular pattern of English speech. In late O.E. a few Scandinavian words had already been adopted; a number, naturally enough, were military terms, most of which have been lost; *griŏ* (peace), *ŏræl* (thrall, slave), *rān* (plunder). Some more common words also belong to this early group, e.g. *take* (which gradually replaced O.E. *niman*), *call, fellow, husband.* But we have to wait till the M.E. period to find a greater number of Scandinavian loan-words and evidence of a considerable influence on M.E. forms and sounds. It will be convenient to discuss these together.

It is not easy to detect any general grouping of the Scand. loan-words similar to what we shall find in words taken from French. They are mixed in character and their adoption seems accidental. Thus we have the word *window*, meaning 'wind-eye', which replaced the O.E. *ēagŏȳrl*, in which the first element also means *eye*, the second part meaning *hole*, the same as our *–tril* in *nostril*. *Sky* is another Scand. borrowing; the O.E. *uprodor* has completely disappeared. Many words with *sk(sc)* are of Scand. origin, e.g. *scant*, *skill*, *skin*, *score*, *bask*, etc. Other miscellaneous words are *ill*, *ugly*, *happy*, *wing*, *(a)loft*, *hit*, *cast*, *till* (preposition) and *fro* (as in *to and fro*).

We frequently find, instead of the replacement of an English word by an entirely different Scand. one (e.g. *sky* for *uprodor*), a modification in the form of the O.E. word caused by the cognate Scand. term. Thus some O.E. words with *g*, pronounced *y*, were changed through the influence of the corresponding Scand. word in which the *g* was pronounced as in *go*. O.E. *giefan* had a sound *y*; this is still shown in Chaucer's *yeve*, *yaf* (give, gave); the Mod. form with *g* is probably due to the Scand. word which had the "hard" sound of g. O.E. *ǽg* (*egg*) gives M.E. *ey*, also found in Chaucer, but our *egg* must have been influenced by Scand. A similar interchange is seen in certain words with O.E. *c*, pronounced *ch*,[1] where the cognate Scand. word had *k*, and O.E. *sc*, pronounced *sh*, where Scand. had *sk*. In these groups two forms have frequently survived, one reflecting the O.E. sound, the other the Scand. Such pairs of words are called doublets. Thus we have Eng. *church*, Scand. *kirk* (this may, however, be explained as a Northern dialect form), *shirt* by the side of Scand. *skirt*, Eng. *shot* (*to pay one's shot*) and Scand. *scot* (*to go scot-free*). Other doublets are seen in Eng. *edge* and Scand. *egg*, as in the phrase *to egg on*, which has nothing to do with the noun *egg*.

Scandinavian influence also operated in another branch of the vocabulary where foreign borrowing is unusual. It is generally held that the three pronouns *they*, *their* and *them* are of Scand. origin and some scholars add *she*, though this is more doubtful. The first three pronouns

[1] See p. 55.

were in O.E. *hi(e)*, *hira*, and *him* or *heom*. Chaucer still uses *hir* and *hem*,[2] descended from these O.E. forms, but he has the Scand. *they*, thus showing, as in so many other features, the transitional nature of his language; ultimately, however, *hir* and *hem* are replaced by *their* and *them*, probably because they were so easily confused with *her* and *him*. The introduction of these *th* forms may also have been helped by the influence of the very similar *th* forms of the definite article, *ðā*, *ðāra*, *ðǣm*, especially as this was often used as a pronoun in O.E. The pronoun *she* may also, at least partly, be due to Scand. influence, though it may be derived to some extent from the feminine definite article *sēo*.

It may be noted that the Scand. language had a considerable effect on English place-names, and the extent to which the Vikings overran the country can be estimated from this evidence. Thus names in –*by* are of Scand. origin; this ending is the Scand. word for a town and corresponds to –*ton* in English place-names. *Whitby*, *Grimsby* (the town of Grim), *Derby*, and many other names contain this word. It may be present in the term *by-law*, originally 'town-law', which should accordingly not be spelt *bye*; the word *law* is also of Scand. origin.

A much more vital part in the development of the language is played by French. This is not surprising when we consider that for about three centuries after the Norman Conquest French was the official language of the country. It was used in the schools, in Parliament, in the law courts, and by other public bodies. It might have become the permanent language of England, or a bilingual system might easily have developed similar to that which prevails in Canada today, but English gradually emerged again, and by the end of the fourteenth century was once more

---

[2] E.g. So priketh *hem* nature in *hir* corages, "so nature incites *them* in *their* hearts."

the dominant tongue. The English language did not vanish completely, however, at any time, even in literature; during the transition period the records are continuous, though between 1000 and 1300 there is not much that is of major literary importance. This relegation of English to a secondary position, and the absence of a strong literary tradition, which always tends towards conservatism, may also help to explain the rapid change in the structure of the language during this transition period.

Relics from this age when French was the official language can still be seen in certain legal and parliamentary formulae. Thus when a bill is signed by the king and becomes the law of the land, he uses the phrase *le Roy le veult* 'the king agrees', which obviously goes back to the French that was current in England at this period. If he disagrees he writes *le Roy avisera*, 'the king will think it over'. Another fossil is seen in the phrase *Oyez!* or *O yes!* used at the opening of Parliament and the law courts and often shouted by the bellman or town crier, who still survives in some of the more remote places in England. This is a distorted form of an old Fr. imperative *oyez*, meaning *listen*, which is much more intelligible at the beginning of an announcement than *O yes!* But these forms, unlike the vast number of Fr. loan-words, are not organic parts of the normal language.

Attempts have been made to estimate the extent to which loan-words from Fr. entered English at different stages of M.E. The latest results show that the period of most rapid absorption was the second half of the fourteenth century, the age of Chaucer. During these fifty years it appears that about twenty per cent of the total Fr. element in the vocabulary passed into the language. The previous half-century (1300–1350) saw the appearance of a large number of Fr. words, but before 1250 very few are found. After 1400 there is also a marked decrease, though, as we shall see, we have continued to adopt words from Fr. right down to our own day. But in contrast to the twenty per cent borrowed between 1350 and 1400 we find only about two per cent before 1200[3] and, in modern times, about two-and-a-half per cent between 1850 and 1900.[4] It might also be noted that an examination of Chaucer's total vocabulary to determine the proportion of native and non-native words has shown that slightly over half are of non-English origin, mainly Fr.[5] If, instead of proceeding in this way, we take a series of passages of considerable length chosen at random and estimate the percentage of non-native words, i.e. we analyse the poet's language "in action", the proportion is much lower, generally less than twenty per cent. In this calculation each word is counted only once; the native words recur of course much more frequently than the others. These percentages may be compared with figures obtained for other later writers; see Chapter 8. Mersand (*op. cit.*) has estimated Chaucer's total working vocabulary as 8,430 words.

These numerous Fr. loan-words can be divided into various classes, which clearly reflect the nature of the influence exerted by the Normans on English life and society. The general tendency is for the basic central elements in the vocabulary to survive from O.E. and for less essential words, especially those of a technical nature and those indicating ideas of luxury, to be borrowed from Fr. This distinction between native English words and the new Fr. borrowings is often illustrated by the dialogue between the swineherd Gurth and the jester Wamba in

[3] Some of these early borrowings are *castle, court, peace, war, prison, treasure.*

[4] For these statistics see Jespersen, *Growth and Structure of the English Language*, p. 94, and Baugh, *A History of the English Language*, p. 219.

[5] See J. Mersand, *Chaucer's Romance Vocabulary*.

Scott's *Ivanhoe*. Wamba calls Gurth's attention to the curious fact that, when animals are alive and have to be tended in the field by the Saxon serf they retain their English names, *swine, ox*, etc., but that when they are slaughtered and served up as meat on the table of the Norman-French overlord, they are given French names, *pork, beef* (cf. *porc, boeuf*). This list can be extended: Eng. *calf*, Fr. *veal* (*veau*), Eng. *deer*, Fr. *venison*, Eng. *sheep*, Fr. *mutton* (*mouton*).[6] Many other groups may be contrasted in the same way. Thus we have the native word *breakfast* (*break+fast*), but the more luxurious meals *dinner*[7] and *supper* with words from Fr. The names of occupations show the same differences; basic trades in mediaeval times such as the *smith, baker, miller, brewer, ploughman* have native words, while *tailor, barber, mason, carpenter* and other occupations less essential in a primitive age are given Fr. names. The most fundamental family relationships preserve their O.E. names, *father, mother, brother, sister*, but *uncle, aunt, niece, nephew, cousin* are taken over from Fr.; *grandfather, grandmother*, etc., are of mixed origin, *grand* being a Fr. word and the second element of the compound English. Words of this type are called hybrids. O.E. had a word for uncle, *ēam*; Chaucer uses both terms, *eem* and *uncle*, even in the same poem (*Troilus and Criseyde*).

Besides these mixed groups there are many categories with a large preponderance of Fr. words. Thus most of our military terms are derived from Fr.; this is not surprising, as the Norman-French imposed their military system on England. We have, for instance, *peace, war, battle*,

---

[6] In this section Fr. loan-words are given in their Mod. E. forms. There is generally not much difference between these and the M.E. words. But the Mod. Fr. forms often show considerable changes, e.g. Eng. *faith*, Mod. Fr. *foi*.

[7] It is interesting to note that the Fr. word *dîner* is derived from a Latin word which meant 'to break one's fast'.

victory, defeat, prison(er), siege, soldier, hostage, army, navy, the various ranks and branches of the army, *officer, general, corporal, sergeant, infantry, artillery, cavalry*. In many cases the O.E. word disappeared; thus O.E. had two words for army, *here* and *fierd*, both of which have been lost, just like *friδ*, 'peace', and *sige*, 'victory', and many other native words. A large number of political and legal terms are also borrowed. The word *parliament* (cf. Fr. *parler*, to speak) replaced the O.E. *witenagemōt*, 'the meeting of the wise men', the nearest approach to a parliament in O.E. times. Similarly, while such essential members of the mediaeval social system as the king and queen retain their O.E. titles, *prince, princess, crown, realm, royal, palace, peer, privy council, nation, people* are of Fr. origin; though *law* is Scand., *judge, jury, verdict, assize, innocent, plaintiff, defendant, sentence* are borrowings from Fr.; *witness* and *guilty* are, however, English. Most of our titles are from Fr.: *sir, sire, Mr.* (a modification of *master*), *Mrs.* and *Miss* (both reduced forms of *mistress—Mistress* for *Mrs.* can still be heard in Scotland and Nova Scotia), *duke, duchess, count(ess), viscount, marquis,* etc.; *earl, lord, lady* are, however, English (O.E. *eorl, hlāford, hlǣfdīge*). Many words used in the arts are found in this Fr. group: *poet(ry), poesy, literature, letters, verse, ballad, comedy, tragedy, music, dance, art(ist), paint(er), colour,* etc. A large number of abstracts have also come over from Fr.: *religion, faith, charity, vice, virtue, purity, chastity, courage, avarice, gluttony, liberty, equality, fraternity,* etc. There are still, of course, many abstract words of O.E. derivation, especially those ending in *–ness, –dom;* thus by the side of *liberty* from Fr. we have Eng. *freedom,* Fr. *bounty,* Eng. *goodness,* though the last two words are no longer synonyms.

It will be noted that these Fr. words, like many others, have conformed to the regular pattern of the English vocabulary, unlike more recent borrowings which retain a Fr. appearance and a would-be-French pronunciation, e.g. *chagrin, naïve, camouflage, ensemble.* In fact some of these M.E. loan-words are so familiar that it is quite surprising to find that they are actually of Fr. origin, e.g. *very, pass, catch, caught, easy, river, poor, use, cry, save, tax, sound, sum, cost, city, face.* These everyday words are exceptions to the general rule suggested above that our basic words are of O.E. origin; they are not in the least exotic.

Generally when two words, one of Eng. and the other of Fr. origin, are found in the language denoting the same idea, the Eng. word is more colloquial, the Fr. one more literary; thus we have *hide* and *conceal, begin* and *commence, building* and *edifice,* etc. This is, however, not always true; for instance *people* from Fr. is a more ordinary word than Eng. *folk,* apart from the colloquial use of *folks.*

Most of these Fr. words are derived from Latin; in addition a number of Lat. words are taken over directly into M.E. Sometimes it is difficult to say whether a word is a Lat. or Fr. borrowing; *religion* thus might come directly from Lat. or through Fr. Occasionally the same Lat. word appears in English in two or three different forms, one close to the original Lat., the others considerably modified in passing through Fr. Examples are *regal* (cf. Lat. *regalis*), *royal; blaspheme, blame; dignity, dainty; legal, loyal,* also dialectal *leal; gentile, gentle,* also later *genteel* and *jaunty; senior* (Lat.), *sire* (Fr.), then later reduced in Eng. to *sir.*

On the whole the loan-words from Lat. in M.E. were of a less popular nature than those from Fr. or the Lat. borrowings in O.E. A few examples are *adjacent, custody, incredible, individual, intellect, scripture, lucrative, necessary, ornate, secular, rational, reject, testimony, tribu-*

tary, though some more common words such as *picture*, *polite* were also adopted.

A small number of words were borrowed in M.E. from languages other than Fr. and Lat., mainly Low German (Dutch), but these may conveniently be considered in the chapter on the Mod. E. vocabulary.

To illustrate Middle English two extracts are given from Chaucer.

THE PRIORESS

From the *Prologue to the Canterbury Tales*

Ther was also a Nonne, a PRIORESSE,
That of hir smyling was ful simple and coy;
Hir gretteste ooth was but by sëynt Loy;
And she was cleped madame Eglentyne.
⁵ Ful wel she song the service divyne,
Entuned in hir nose ful semely;
And Frensh she spak ful faire and fetisly,
After the scole of Stratford atte Bowe,
For Frensh of Paris was to hir unknowe.
¹⁰ At mete wel y-taught was she with-alle;
She leet no morsel from hir lippes falle,
Ne wette hir fyngres in hir sauce depe.
Wel coude she carie a morsel, and wel kepe,
That no drope ne fille up-on hir brest.
¹⁵ In curteisye was set ful muche hir lest.
Hir over lippe wyped she so clene,
That in hir coppe was no ferthing sene
Of grece, whan she dronken hadde hir draughte.
Ful semely after hir mete she raughte,

L.2 coy, 'quiet'. l.4 cleped, 'called'. l.7 fetisly, 'elegantly'. ll. 10, 19 mete, 'food'. l.14 fille, 'fell'. l.15 was set ful muche hir lest, 'she was very keen on'. l.17 ferthing, 'spot'. l.19 raughte, 'reached'.

20 And sikerly she was of greet disport,
   And ful pleasunt, and amiable of port,
   And peyned hir to countrefete chere
   Of court, and been estatlich of manere,
   And to ben holden digne of reverence.
25 But, for to speken of hir conscience,
   She was so charitable and so pitous,
   She wolde wepe, if that she sawe a mous
   Caught in a trappe, if it were deed or bledde.
   Of smale houndes had she, that she fedde
30 With rosted flesh, or milk and wastel-breed.
   But sore weep she if oon of hem were deed,
   Or if men smoot it with a yerde smerte:
   And al was conscience and tendre herte.
   Ful semely hir wimpel pinched was;
35 Hir nose tretys; hir eyen greye as glas;
   Hir mouth ful smal, and ther-to softe and reed;
   But sikerly she hadde a fair forheed;
   It was almost a spanne brood, I trowe;
   For, hardily, she was nat undergrowe.
40 Ful fetis was hir cloke, as I was war.
   Of smal coral aboute hir arm she bar
   A peire of bedes, gauded al with grene;
   And ther-on heng a broche of gold ful shene,
   On which ther was first write a crowned A,
45 And after, *Amor vincit omnia*.

From Chaucer's "Retraction" to the *Canterbury Tales*.

Now preye I to hem alle that herkne this litel tretys

L.20 sikerly, 'certainly'; of greet disport, 'easily amused'.
l.21 port, 'behaviour'. l.22 chere, 'behaviour'. l.23 estatlich, 'stately'.
l.24 digne, 'worthy'. l.29 houndes, 'dogs'. l.30 wastel-breed, 'bread
made of fine flour'. l.32 yerde, 'rod'. l.35 tretys, 'well-shaped'.
l.40 fetis, 'neat'. l.42 a peire of bedes, 'a rosary'; gauded al with
grene, 'with a green one after every ten'. l.43 shene, 'beautiful'.
l.45 *Amor vincit omnia*, 'Love conquers everything'.

or rede, that if ther be any thyng in it that liketh hem, that therof they thanken oure Lord Jhesu Crist, of whom procedeth al wit and al goodnesse, and if ther be any thyng that displese hem, I preye hem also that they arrette it to the defaute of myn unkonnynge, and nat to my wyl, that wolde ful fayn have seyd bettre if I hadde had konnynge. For oure book seith, "Al that is writen is writen for oure doctrine", and that is myn entente. Wherfore I biseke yow mekely, for the mercy of God, that ye preye for me that Crist have mercy on me and foryeve me my giltes; and namely of my translacions and enditynges of worldly vanitees, the whiche I revoke in my retracciouns . . . . thanke I oure Lord Jhesu Crist and his blisful Mooder, and alle the seintes of hevene bisekynge hem that they from hennes forth unto my lyves ende sende me grace to biwayle my giltes, and to studie to the salvacioun of my soule and graunte me grace of verray penitence, confessioun and satisfaccioun to doon in this present lyf, thurgh the benigne grace of hym that is kyng of kynges and preest over alle preestes, that boghte us with the precious blood of his herte; so that I may be oon of hem at the day of doom that shulle be saved.

Arrette, 'ascribe'; unkonnynge, 'ignorance'; entente, 'intention'; verray, 'true'.

7. The Structure of Middle English

SOUNDS AND SPELLINGS

The question of the development of O.E. sounds in M.E. is complicated by the fact that, as has been already explained, we pass from one dialect (West Saxon) to another (E. Midl.) and, further, because the spelling sometimes conceals changes in sounds and sometimes, on the other hand, suggests changes that have not actually taken place. Thus, for instance, when O.E. *ū* as in *hūs* appears as *ou* in M.E. *hous* it might naturally be thought that this reflects a sound-change and that the *ou* of the M.E. spelling indicates the modern sound of the *ou* in *house*. Actually, however, the sound of *ū* remained unchanged in the M.E. period, certainly in early M.E., and the new spelling of *ou* is due to the influence of Fr., where even today *ou* represents the sound *u*, as in *rouge*, *vous*, etc. In words like *through*, *uncouth*, *group* this *ou* still preserves its M.E. value in Mod. E.

Unlike other departments of the language, sounds show little change between the O.E. and M.E. periods, far less than between M.E. and Mod. E. The most important are two changes in the vowels, O.E. *ā* (as in *hām*, home) and *ȳ* (as in *hȳdan*, hide) or *y* (as in *synn*, sin). O.E. *ā* started on its path towards Mod. *o*; it has in M.E. an intermediate sound, about the same as in Mod. *saw*, and is often written *oo*, which must not be pronounced like *oo* in *soon*. Thus we find:

O.E.	M.E.
hām, bān, āc, stān	hoom, boon, ook, stoon
	(pron. hawm, bawn, awk, stawn)

Mod. E.
home, bone, oak, stone

This change does not appear in the Northern dialect; there O.E. ā moves in a different direction, leading to hame, stane, etc., forms which are used in the Scottish vernacular by writers like Burns[1] and Scott and can still be heard in certain dialects in Scotland.

In the E. Midl. dialect of M.E., O.E. ȳ and y became ī and i, and are levelled under these two sounds from O.E.; all four produce Mod. E. "long i" and "short i". The spelling y is often retained in M.E., but it no longer indicates the sound in Fr. lune as it did in O.E. Thus O.E. hȳdan may appear in M.E. as hyde(n), but the y must now be pronounced like ee in see. O.E. synn, pytt may still be written in this way in M.E., but the pronunciation is the same as Mod. sin, pit.

The O.E. diphthongs were simplified in M.E. Thus O.E. ēo became ē (as in lay) and eo became e, e.g. O.E. dēop becomes dep(e), pronounced approximately dape, O.E. eorl becomes erl with the sound of e in let. The other O.E. diphthongs, ea and ie, are similarly reduced to single vowels.

There is little change in the consonants. The O.E. groups cn–, gn–, wr–, etc., are still preserved. In certain words O.E. g becomes w, e.g. O.E. boga > M.E. bowe (bow and arrow), sorg > sorwe (sorrow), lagu (Scand.) > law, etc. In many other cases what looks like a change of sound is merely, as we shall see, a spelling change.

---

[1] Cf. Burns: His clean hearth-stane, his thrifty wifie's smile.

M.E. Spelling

M.E. orthography was greatly influenced by French. We have already mentioned the substitution of *ou* for *u* as an example of this. In another group of words O.E. *u* had its spelling changed to *o*; this, however, is not due to Fr. spelling, but was intended to make it easier to read the words. This *o* is seen in words like *come, love, son*, where O.E. had *cuman, lufu, sunu*; the *u* sound persisted in M.E. One letter, O.E. *æ*, was gradually dropped in M.E., and replaced generally by *a*.

In the consonants Fr. modes of spelling show themselves in the new symbol *qu* where O.E. had the more phonetic *cw*; thus O.E. *cwēn, cwic, cwellan* begin to be spelt *queen, quick, quell*, a quite unnecessary addition to the English alphabet, as *cw* or *kw* are unambiguous symbols. The use of *k* for the sound in *king* (O.E. *cyning*), which had started in O.E., becomes more common in M.E. before certain vowels, *c* being retained before others. O.E. *c* in many words is now spelt *ch*, O.E. *cirice*, M.E. *church*, etc., and O.E. *sc* is now often spelt *sh*, O.E. *fisc*, M.E. *fish*, O.E. *sceal, sceolde*, M.E. *shal, sholde*. O.E. *g*, pronounced *y* in a large group of words, is gradually written *y*, O.E. *gēar*, M.E. *yeer*; it sometimes disappeared altogether, as in O.E. *gif, genoh*, M.E. *if, enough*. This *y* sound was often written with a symbol ʒ in M.E. This was confused with *z* and this confusion explains such strange Mod. spellings as *Dalziell* with the *z* still often pronounced with a *y*-sound, *capercailzie*, etc. The letter *z* is introduced from Fr.; in O.E. *s* had this sound as well as the normal sound of *s*. The sounds of *f* and *v* are gradually indicated by two letters instead of one (*f*) in O.E.[2] A new letter *j* (written *i* until the sixteenth century or

[2] See p. 56.

even later) is seen in words like *juge* (judge), and it or *gg* replaces the O.E. *cg* which had this sound, e.g. O.E. *brycg*, M.E. *brigge* (Mod. *bridge*), O.E. *ecg*, M.E. *egge*, Mod. *edge*. The two O.E. symbols ð and þ are replaced in M.E. by *th*; a trace of þ survives, as we have seen, in the mock antique *ye olde*, where þ was confused with *y*. The two sounds of *h* as in O.E. *niht* and *genoh* are generally written *gh* (*nyght*, *ynough*) as in Mod. E.

Lengthening and Shortening of Vowels

A number of interesting changes affecting the length of vowels, which have left many traces in Mod. E., occur in late O.E. and early M.E. Sometimes an original short vowel is lengthened; more often a long vowel is shortened. This explains the presence in Mod. E. of such pairs of words as *child–children*, *goose–gosling*, *hide–hid* ,*clean– cleanly* (also *cleanse*), etc. Certain groups of consonants have the effect of lengthening a preceding vowel; thus *nd*, *mb* cause O.E. *findan*, *climban* to become *fīndan*, *clīmban*, and this *ī*, still pronounced like *ee* in *see* in M.E., ultimately becomes Mod. E. "long *i*". Similarly, O.E. *cild* becomes *cīld* (Mod. *child*). But when this *ld* was followed by *r* as in the plural *cildru* the three consonants *ldr* kept the vowel short, and so we have *children* with short *i*. Other consonant combinations cause shortening of vowels, e.g. *sl*, *sw*, *sb*, *fth*, *pt*, *dd*, *nl*, *ns*, etc. This explains such pairs as *goose* (O.E. *gōs*), *gosling* (M.E. *gōs+ling*), *house* (O.E. *hūs*), *husband*, *five* (O.E. *fīf*), *fifth*, *keep* (O.E. *cēpan*), *kept* (O.E. *cēpte*), *hide* (O.E. *hȳdan*), *hid*, etc. Vowels were also frequently shortened in unaccented syllables, especially endings. Compare O.E. *dōm*, M.E. *doom*, and the ending *–dom* with its slurred vowel. These two shortening processes explain an interesting development of the word *hūswīf* (=housewife): the *ū* was shortened before *sw*; the *ī* was shortened because of its unstressed position; the sounds of *w* and *f* were also lost because of lack of stress, and, as a result, *hūswīf* becomes, surprisingly, Mod. E. *hussy*. This is also a good example of degeneration in the meaning of a word, a process that will be discussed in Chapter 10. Another form of the word, not so much reduced as *hussy* either in form or meaning, is seen in the sailor's term *housewife*, sometimes pronounced *huzif*, a receptacle for needles, pins, etc.

FORMS IN M.E.

The forms of the noun and adjective, so numerous and complex in O.E., are reduced in M.E. almost to the point they have reached in Mod. E. The verbs and the pronouns are not simplified quite so much.

The Noun

Of the many types of nouns in O.E. very few are left in M.E., and in those that survive the number of forms is scarcely greater than today. If we compare the O.E. paradigm of *hund* (p. 60) with M.E. we find only two or three forms left.

	Singular	*Plural*
Nom., Acc.	hound	houndes
Genitive	houndes	"
Dative	hounde (rare)	

If we disregard the dative, which is occasionally found in M.E., it will be seen that the only surviving ending is the *–es*, which corresponds to Mod. *–s*. The process of simplification is practically complete.

There are still a number of nouns in M.E. that do not make their plural in *s*. The *–en* plurals are more common than in Mod. E.; in fact at one period, especially in the Southern dialect, this so-called weak plural seemed to be gaining ground. Chaucer has a number of these plurals in words which in Mod. E. have the normal *s* ending, e.g. *eyen*, *eyne* (still found in one or two places in Shakespeare), *toon* (also *toos*), 'toes', *foon*, 'foes', *been*, 'bees', *asshen*, 'ashes', etc. The three Mod. E. plurals in *–n*, *children*, *brethren*, *kine* do not belong to this *n*-declension in O.E., but joined it only in M.E.; the O.E. plurals were *cildru*, *brōðru* and *cȳ*, which should have given Mod. E. *childer*, *brother* and *ky(e)*. Both *childer* and *kye* as plurals are recorded in English dialects, especially in the North.[3] But in M.E. these forms did not look like plurals, and so they changed over to the *n*-pattern. Chaucer has *brethren*, *children* and *keen*. It will be seen that these words really contain a double plural; *childer* already has one plural ending *–er*, and to this is added a second *–(e)n*. The plural of O.E. *cū* (cow) is *cȳ* (kye), just as that of *mūs* (mouse) is *mȳs* (mice); here again a second plural has been added. The Mod. form *cows* is of course a new formation on the analogy of the normal plural in *s*; it rarely occurs before 1600.

The *s*-less genitive of this weak declension is occasionally found in M.E., e.g. in Chaucer's line:

> In hope to stonden in his *lady* grace

where we should write *lady's* in Mod. E.; the Chaucerian form comes from O.E. *hlǣfdīgan*; cf. Mod. E., *Lady Day*.

The unchanged plural (*sheep*, *deer*) is also more wide-

---

[3] Cf. Burns: The *kye* stood rowtin i' the loan, or: His sheep an' *kye* thrive bonie, O.

spread than in Mod. E. Thus Chaucer has *hors* as a plural, as can be seen from the line:

His *hors were* goode, but he was nat gay,

where the verb *were* and the adjective *goode* show that *hors* is plural. He also uses *yeer* as a plural:

Of twenty *yeer* of age he was, I gesse.

In other places, however, he has *yeres*. Both these words have adopted the regular s-pattern in Mod. E. (*horses*, *years*).

The Adjective

Of the extremely complex declension of the O.E. adjective (see Ch. 5) only a single trace is left, the ending *–e*. The rules for its use are very simple and can be observed in Chaucer. It is attached to the adjective when the noun is plural:

And *smale fowles* maken melodye.

It is also found when the adjective is preceded by a word such as *the, this, that, his, her*, etc., e.g. the *yonge* sonne, 'the young sun', his *halfe* cours, 'half his course'. This final *–e* has been dropped in Mod. E. (*small, half, young*).

One other difference in the M.E. adjective is the occasional change of vowel shown in the comparative and superlative. This still survives in *old, elder, eldest*, but in O.E. and M.E. it was more common. Thus Chaucer has

long	lenger	lengest
strong	strenger	strengest

He has also other forms that differ from Mod. E. and are closer to O.E., e.g. *fer, ferrer, ferrest* for *far, farther, farthest*.

The Definite Article

The dozen or more forms of the O.E. definite article are reduced in M.E. to the one word *the*. The disappearance of the inflections of the adjective and definite article is closely connected with the change from grammatical gender to logical gender which also marks the M.E. period.

The Adverb

The O.E. adverbial ending *–līce* appears in M.E. as *–liche* and *–ly*; thus Chaucer has both *royalliche* and *royally*. He also uses a number of adverbs in *–e*, some of which have gone over in Mod. E. to the *–ly* class, e.g. *smerte* (smartly), *brighte* (bright or brightly); cf. Mod. E. the sun shines *bright(ly)*.

The Verb

There is less change in the M.E. verb than in the noun or adjective. A comparison between the principal parts of the verbs in O.E. and M.E. shows the following differences:

STRONG VERBS

	Infinitive	*Past Sing.*
Class 1	O.E. rīdan	rād
	M.E. ride(n)	rood
Class 3	O.E. singan	sang, song
	M.E. singe(n)	sang, song

Past Plural	*Past Participle*
O.E. ridon	(ge)riden
M.E. riden	(y)ride(n)
O.E. sungon	(ge)sungen
M.E. sungen	(y)sung(e)(n), (y)song(en)

WEAK VERBS

	Infinitive	*Past Sing.*
Class 1	O.E. hīeran	hīerde
	M.E. here(n)	herde
	O.E. sēcan	sōhte
	M.E. seke(n)	so(u)ghte
Class 2	O.E. lufian	lufode
	M.E. love(n)	lovede

Past Plural	*Past Participle*
O.E. hīerdon	(ge)hīered
M.E. herden	(y)herd
O.E. sōhton	(ge)sōht
M.E. so(u)ghten	(y)so(u)ght
O.E. lufodon	(ge)lufod
M.E. loveden	(y)loved

The M.E. forms fluctuate considerably, even in the same author. Thus Chaucer sometimes drops the *y*– or the –*n* of the past participle or the –*n* of the infinitive; sometimes he retains these sounds; in this respect as in so many others, M.E. is in a transition state. In the *Prologue to the Canterbury Tales* we find infinitives such as *seken* (to seek), *speken*, but also *falle, kepe, wepe, ryde* (to ride), past participles such as *holpen* (helped), *dronken*, but also *yronne* (run), *ytaught*.

The O.E. present participle in –*ende* has been replaced in Chaucer, as in Mod. E., by –*ing* (–*yng*, –*ynge*). In other M.E. dialects and writers, however, we find –*ande*, –*ende* and –*inde*. A special form of the imperative plural still shows itself occasionally, as in O.E.; in Mod. E. we have only one imperative form. Thus Chaucer writes: *Cometh neer*, 'Come near'. But he uses the uninflected imperative as well.

A number of verbs which were strong in O.E. have become weak in M.E. and Mod. E., and a few verbs have moved in the other direction. Often, however, the M.E. verb still follows the O.E. pattern. We find, for instance, strong forms in Chaucer like *clomb* (Mod. climbed) from O.E. *clomb*, *halp*, *holpen* (helped), *carf* (carved), *swal* (swelled), etc. But *bake*, which in O.E. was strong—*bacan*, *bōc*, *bacen*—and should normally have developed the same pattern as *shake* and given us *bake*, *book*, *baken*, is generally weak in Chaucer with a past tense *baked(e)*. O.E. *faran*, a strong verb, is also weak; O.E. *lēosan*, M.E. *lese* (lose), whose past tense was *lēas* in O.E., has become weak (*loste*). In some verbs Chaucer has both weak and strong forms of the past, e.g. *sleep* (strong past from O.E. *slēp*) and *slepte*, *weep* and *wepte*.

In *werede* he shows a weak form which has become strong (*wore*) in Mod. E. Another example of the rare change from a weak to a strong pattern is seen in Mod. *dig*, *dug*, where an earlier *digged* is found in M.E.

The Pronouns

Some of the most important changes in the pronouns have already been indicated in discussing the Scand. element in M.E., namely the introduction of the new pronouns *they*, *their* and *them*.[4] We may also note the disappearance of the O.E. accusative singular pronouns *hine* and *hie*, for which the datives *him* and *her* are substituted. The new feminine *she*, whose origin is uncertain, has replaced O.E. *hēo*, though traces of this latter pronoun long persisted in the dialects and can be heard in the Northern *hoo* (she) today. *Ye* and *you* (*yow*), *thou* (*thow*) and *thee* are still in common use, though *ye* and *you* are beginning to be employed in addressing a single person, thus

[4] See p. 76.

pointing to the Mod. use of *you* for both singular and plural. The Mod. forms of the relative pronouns, *who*, *which* and *that*, emerge in M.E. In O.E. the definite article or the pronoun of the third person (*hē, hēo, hit*) or an indeclinable *ðe* were used as relatives. Now we begin to find our Mod. relatives, though not yet specialized as in Mod. E., *who* referring to a person, *which* to things, and *that* to either persons or things. Chaucer often uses *which* to refer to a person; his usual relative is, however, *that*.

SYNTAX

Several of the features noted in O.E. syntax persist in M.E., for instance the repeated negative.

An interesting syntactical development in M.E. is the new mode of indicating possession with *of*, which provides the language with two means of showing this relationship. In O.E. it was shown by the genitive ending *–es, –an*, etc., e.g. *eorles helm*, 'the warrior's helmet'. In this phrase M.E. and Mod. usage follows O.E., but in a phrase like *sweordes ecg* we should prefer to say 'the edge *of the sword*' rather than '*the sword's edge*'. This new construction with *of* is probably due to the French method of using *de* to show possession, and is thus an example of Fr. influence on syntax.

The subjunctive is still common in M.E. Chaucer has sentences such as: I shal *felen* (feel) what he *mene* (means) or: For man sholde avyse what he *speeke*, 'For one should be careful of what he *says*'.

Impersonal constructions are more frequent in M.E. than in Mod. E., e.g. *me were levere dye*, lit. 'It were better for me to die', where we should say 'I would rather die'. This phrase shows another use of the subjunctive *were*. Expressions such as *me thinketh, me thoghte, hem thoghte* (it seems, seemed to me, seemed to them) show a M.E. idiom descended from O.E. (*me ðynceð*, etc.) and still found in archaic Mod. E. *methinks, methought.*

In questions we can see the gradual development of the auxiliary *do, did.* Thus Chaucer says, on the one hand, *Seyde he nat thus?* (*lit.* Said he not thus?), reflecting the O.E. usage, and also *Fader, why do ye wepe?,* which shows the Mod. construction with *do.* In negative phrases he still generally follows the O.E. practice, e.g. *It cordeth naught,* 'it does not agree', or *Blameth nat me,* 'do not blame me!'

A relative is often omitted in M.E. where it is essential in Mod. E. syntax, for instance, in Chaucer's sentence:

> With hym ther was a Plowman, was his brother,

where we must supply *who* in a modern translation.

A feature of O.E. syntax that is still noticeable in M.E. is the occasional omission of a verb indicating motion. Examples from Chaucer are:

> And some man wolde out of his prisoun fayn
> (And some man would gladly [go] out of his prison)

or

> That day by day to scole was his wone.
> (Who day by day used [to go] to school.)

Another omission not infrequently found in Chaucer is the absence of the word *of,* where it is required in the modern idiom, e.g. She was, as it were, *a manner deye* (a sort *of* dairymaid); the beste *galon wyn* (gallon *of* wine).

Chaucerian syntax is, on the whole, fairly close to our modern usage. Especially in word-order the language has travelled a long way from O.E. and has developed to a great extent the habits of the speech of today.

8.   The Modern Period

In the modern period (1500 to the present day) most of the tendencies which showed themselves in M.E. are still in operation. Changes in sounds are even more extensive; the forms move further in the direction of simplicity and uniformity; the borrowing of words, no longer restricted to those of French, Scandinavian and Latin origin, continues on a large scale, with practically every language of importance now making its contribution; syntax develops on the whole an even more regular pattern. There is nothing in Mod. E. quite comparable to the far-reaching influence of French in M.E., but such great movements as the Renaissance and the modern developments of science and technology have had important effects on the language.

THE VOCABULARY

With the modern age we arrive at the greatest period of expansion in the English vocabulary. An ever-increasing number of foreign languages are drawn upon, and gradually the abundant and composite stock of words is accumulated. The arguments for and against this method of extending the vocabulary of a language have already been discussed in Chapter 2; in this chapter we shall watch the process at work.

Borrowings from Latin and Greek

Under the influence of the Renaissance a large number of words were adopted from classical languages during the early modern period, not always with the happiest results. The scholars and writers of the sixteenth and seventeenth centuries seemed to be intoxicated by this newly awakened interest in classical literature and, as we shall see in connection with spelling, tried to carry over some of its qualities into English. As a result they introduced, freely but not always very judiciously, many words of classical origin and attempted to naturalize them in the language. There are two opposite tendencies at work during this period: one group of writers wished to keep English as free as possible from these borrowed words; the other, in their enthusiasm for the classics, wanted to draw generously on the resources of Latin and Greek. Many of the words which the latter group tried to introduce have fortunately died out; others have proved to be useful and have survived. Examples of words from these languages that have not found a home in our language can be seen in many authors of this age. Thus at the end of the fifteenth century Caxton, who introduced printing into England, attempts to bring in such words as *excidyon,* Lat. *excidium,* 'siege', *exercite,* Lat. *exercitus,* 'army'. In the sixteenth century we find *allect* (to entice), *applicate, adminiculation, canicular* (*canicular days*=dog days), *effectuate* and other polysyllabic words. In the seventeenth century Sir Thomas Browne has *improperations* (reproaches), *incurvate, ossuary, diuturnity,* etc., Milton writes *inquisiturient* (eager to act as an inquisitor), *elenchs* (fallacies), *subdichotomies* (subdivisions), etc. The anti-classical school of the sixteenth century coined the vivid phrase "ink-horn term" for words of this type, and, as can be seen, most of them did not take root in the language. But it is always difficult to prophesy in such matters. We find, for instance, one opponent of this tendency criticizing such words as *industry, maturity, temperance*, another attacking *ingenuity, artificiality, notoriety, negotiation*. In the long run the language seems to assimilate those words which have a useful function to fulfil and to reject most of the others.

One rather unfortunate result of this influx of Latin words in late M.E. and early Mod. E. is the frequent cleavage in form and origin between a noun and the adjective associated with it. Thus we have *eye* and *optical* (cf. Lat. *opticus*), *moon* and *lunar* (cf. Lat. *luna*), *sun* and *solar* (cf. Lat. *sol*), *house* and *domestic* (cf. Lat. *domus*), *uncle* and *avuncular*. Sometimes, however, an adjective of Eng. origin and one derived from Lat. are both available, e.g. *sunny* by the side of *solar, fatherly* and *paternal, motherly* and *maternal*, etc.

After the first effects of the Renaissance weakened to some extent in the seventeenth century, the rate of flow of classical words tended to decrease, and those that were borrowed were less extravagant in their nature. Many of the modern loan-words from Lat. and Gk. are to be found in the sciences. These new coinages generally consist of two roots which were not necessarily found in combination in the language from which they were borrowed, but which have been put together in English to denote a certain field of scientific enquiry, e.g. *eugenics*, built up in the nineteenth century from a Greek root *eu–* meaning *good* and *gen–* meaning *to produce*, or the numerous compounds with *psycho–* such as *psychometry*, etc. Other words such as *geology, geography, philology, psychology* existed as compounds before they were introduced into English. The popular term *ideology* (from Gk. *via* Fr.) goes back to 1796. In *thermonuclear* we find a combination of Greek and Latin.

A number of words have been taken over from Lat. and Gk. in their original form, and some of these cause difficulty owing to their abnormal plural endings; they still follow the classical pattern instead of conforming to the Eng. plural. Examples from Gk. are: *criterion, phenomenon* (plural in *–a*), *crisis, thesis,* etc. (plural *crises, theses*). From Lat. we have such words as *formula, alumna* (plural *–ae*), *alumnus, focus, locus* (plural *–i*), *index, appendix* (plural *–ices,* also *–xes*), *genus* (plural *genera*), *continuum, datum, memorandum, stratum, quantum* (plural *–a*). There is some fluctuation in usage in these words, and the retention of the non-English plurals is of very doubtful value; it would be better if they all adopted the normal Eng. plural ending *–s.* Other classical words and phrases do not present this problem, e.g. *omnibus* (though *omnibi* has been used, perhaps humorously, as a plural), *quota, quorum, alibi, libido, vice versa, viva voce, recipe, psyche,* etc.

Borrowings from French

The Fr. words borrowed during this period can generally be distinguished without much difficulty from the M.E. loan-words. They conform less to the general pattern of the language. Their pronunciation reflects Fr. rather than Eng. speech habits. Thus if we take a modern borrowing like *machine* we note three points in which it reveals its Fr. origin: (1) the pronunciation of *ch* as *sh*; (2) the sounding of *i* as *ee*; (3) the accentuation of the last syllable. In Fr. words taken over in the M.E. period *ch* is pronounced as *tsh*, e.g. *change, chamber,* "long *i*" has the sound heard in *price, prime,* and the accent generally falls on the root syllable, as in *courage, nature.* Typical Mod. Fr. loans are *chagrin* (note the *ch* sound and the accent on the second syllable), words in *–et(te), –esque, –oon,*

–ade, etc. with the accent on the last syllable, e.g. *cadet, coquette, picturesque, grotesque, buffoon, balloon, promenade, parade.*

In recent times there has been a tendency to adopt Fr. words in order to add what is supposed to be social distinctiveness to writing and conversation. These terms may be grouped under headings[1] such as "Society French", e.g. *deb(utante)*, from which a new form *sub-deb* has been coined, *fiancé(e), divorcée, soignée, musicale, boudoir, de luxe*, "Dressmaker's French", e.g. *ensemble* (also used as a musical term), *chic, corsage, lingerie, toilette, décolleté, coiffure, brassière, negligé(e), trousseau*, etc., "Culinary French", e.g. *table d'hôte, à la carte, menu, hors d'œuvre, demi-tasse, pie à la mode, entrée*, etc., "Artistic French", e.g. *décor, dénouement, chef d'œuvre, atelier, genre, montage*, etc. "Diplomatic French", the result of the employment of French, until recently, as the official language of diplomacy, has given us *démarche, entente, aide-mémoire, fait accompli, coup*, etc. Some of these words are no longer the usual terms employed in France, for instance *menu*; others are pseudo-French, for instance *pie à la mode*, an expression that would certainly puzzle a Frenchman; both the dish and the term for it are of North American origin. *Nom de plume* (pen-name) is an English-built phrase; the genuine Fr. term is *nom de guerre; double entendre* is not normal Fr., nor is the current use of *morale* in the sense of courage, mental discipline. Other Fr. words of a more general and useful nature have been introduced in modern times, e.g. *camouflage*, now used both literally and figuratively, *garage, defeatism*, etc.: the first two clearly show by their pronunciation their recent adoption from Fr.

It is unfortunate that in Mod. E. we cannot agree to

[1] See G. P. Krapp, *Modern English*, p. 254.

naturalize these Fr. words and spell and pronounce them in the English fashion. The accented letters –é(e), â, ï, do not belong to the English spelling system and the attempts to give a Fr. pronunciation to a word usually result in something that is neither genuine Fr. nor Eng. It would be better and more in accordance with the traditions of our language to make *garage* one hundred per cent English and let it rime with *carriage*, to stop trying to pronounce two nasal vowels in *ensemble*, an impossible task for most English speakers, and in any case, even if successful, an undesirable disturbance to normal English speech-habits. Why not sound the *en* as in *hen* and the *em* as in *them*, as we do in *resemble, assemble*? The usual pronunciation *onsomble* is neither Eng. nor Fr. *Envelope* is gradually becoming Anglicized, though older people still sometimes say *on–*. This linguistic snobbery, both in the use of unnecessary Fr. and pseudo-Fr. words and in their pronunciation, is a harmless but rather childish habit, which one hopes will not spread too far.

Borrowings from German

Most of the Ger. words in the language were borrowed in late Mod. E., mainly in the nineteenth century. A few, however, are earlier, some, chiefly religious terms, going back to the period of the Reformation (sixteenth century). The most important of these is the word *Protestant*, though this may be of either Fr. or Ger. origin. Another interesting early Ger. borrowing is *carouse*, from Ger. *gar aus* (*trinken*), '(drink) up'. Three different types of Ger. loan-words may be distinguished according to the form in which they appear in English. These are: (1) direct adoption without change of form, e.g. *Kindergarten, Hinterland, Wanderlust, Angst*, etc.; (2) the substitution of a cognate English expression, e.g. *loan-word*, the two elements of which are the exact English equivalents of the Ger. *Lehnwort, swan song* (=Ger. *Schwanengesang*); (3) the translation of the Ger. term by Eng. words quite unrelated in form and origin, e.g. *Kriegspiel*, 'war-game', *Schrecklichkeit*, 'frightfulness', *Blitzkrieg*, 'lightning war'. It will be noted that in Classes 2 and 3 the actual words are not Ger.; it is rather the idea behind the Ger. expression that has been transferred and given an Eng. form. This is similar to the process by which Latin words were Anglicized in O.E.; see Ch. 4.

From the point of view of cultural influence we note that Ger. has contributed a large number of words to our philosophical and scientific vocabulary. Many minerals have names of Ger. origin; *zinc, cobalt, bismuth, nickel, feldspar*, etc. are some of the most familiar. In philosophy and psychology Ger. has provided us with many terms, mostly through the third process described above, the free adaptation of a Ger. expression; in some cases the Eng. word was previously in the language but had not been used in the new sense. Examples from philosophy are *æsthetic(s), subjective, objective, transcendental(ism), determinism, pragmatism*, etc. In psychology most of the terminology of psycho-analysis is naturally of Ger. origin: *complex, introvert, extravert, sublimation, narcissism, masochism*, etc. These words all follow an Eng. pattern, and several of them were found in earlier English, but in the new term *Gestalt-psychology* the Ger. word has been taken over unchanged (Process 1 above). In other sciences, too, Ger. has made additions to our vocabulary, e.g. *overtone, chromosome, dynamo, bacillus, relativity, stratosphere*.

Some political and military terms have also been introduced from Ger.: *State socialism, Social Democrat, class-conscious, Nazi(sm)*, an abbreviation of *Nationalsozialist, putsch, Gestapo*, an abbreviation of *ge(heime) Sta(ats) po(lizei)* =Secret State Police, *Führer, Gauleiter*, a provincial political "boss", *U-boat, Zeppelin, Lebensraum* (living-space).

A number of articles of food, originally indigenous to Germany, have brought with them their native names: *sauerkraut, pretzel, hock* (a shortening of *hockamore*, an anglicization of *Hochheimer*), *lager, delicatessen* (adopted in Ger. from Fr. *délicatesse*). Interesting miscellaneous words are *self-portrait, world-famous, epoch-making, folk-song, chain-smoker* (Kettenraucher), *eternal feminine*, (das ewige Weibliche). Occasionally a Ger. term is misinterpreted; the use of *psychological moment*, for instance, is due to a misunderstanding of the Ger. original, which meant a psychological *factor* and had nothing to do with time.

It will be noted that a large proportion of these Ger. loans are compound words.

Other Modern Borrowings

Only a brief indication of the many other languages from which Mod. E. has adopted words can be given.[2] The Dutch language has contributed a number of terms, especially in the departments of shipping and art. In the seventeenth century, when the Dutch were a great nautical people, several words connected with the sea and ships were borrowed. Examples are *boom, sloop, cruise*, all introduced in this century, and *yacht* and *skipper* somewhat earlier. The great achievements of the Dutch and Flemish school of painting are reflected in loan-words such as *easel* (from a Dutch word meaning an ass—cf. *horse* in "Clothes-horse"), *etch* (originally Ger.), *maulstick, landscape, sketch*. A number of words more common in the U.S.A. than in England are also of Dutch origin: *stoop, cookie*

---

[2] For a comprehensive treatment of this part of the subject see L. P. Smith, *The English Language* (Home University Library).

(also used in Scotland), *cole-slaw, boss, boodle, caboose,* and possibly the word *dollar*.[3]

A curious case of the misinterpretation of a Dutch expression is seen in our phrase, *a forlorn hope*. This is a wrong translation of the Dutch *verloren hoop*, where *hoop* means not *hope* but *heap* or *troop*, referring to a band of soldiers sent out with the knowledge that they were doomed.

From the Romance languages other than Fr.—Italian, Spanish, etc.—we have not derived any contribution to our vocabulary at all comparable to that given us by Fr. itself, but a number of interesting and picturesque words have been borrowed from these languages. Many Sp. terms have come, not directly, but by way of India or America, e.g. *alligator, cannibal, hurricane, canoe, mulatto,* a group that brings to mind early ages of exploration and danger. Other more direct loans are a few words connected with bull-fighting such as *matador, toreador,* etc., and *bolero, grandee, desperado, junta, ambuscade, renegade, comrade* (perhaps through Fr.), *siesta, cigar* (from which was formed later *cigarette*), *cork, sherry,* an example of a number of Eng. words derived from names of places, in this case Xeres or Jeres (originally *sherris*). A modern Sp. loan, more common in North America than in England, is *cafeteria,* though some authorities derive this from Italian.

Italian has given us an important group of words belonging to the arts, especially music. Many of our musical terms are of Italian origin, often unchanged in Eng. Thus there are the different types of voices: *soprano, contralto, coloratura,* etc., names of instruments, *piano, violin, viola,*

[3] The contributions of German and Dutch to the language are discussed in two S.P.E. (Society for Pure English) tracts, *The German Influence on the English Vocabulary*, by C. T. Carr, and *The Dutch Influence on the English Vocabulary*, by G. N. Clark. I am indebted to these two works for much of the material included here.

'cello, short for *violoncello,* etc., *aria, scherzo* (=jest, sport), *sonata, prima donna,* and *maestro,* which is rapidly losing its distinctiveness and is being applied, half humorously, to almost any performer, e.g. *a hockey maestro.* The art of painting also reflects a similar influence; *fresco, cameo, studio, mezzotint* are a few of the Ital. terms in this field. Other interesting words from Ital. are *cicerone, fiasco* (meaning in Ital. a bottle, perhaps getting its Eng. meaning from the idea of an empty bottle), *influenza* (originally meaning 'influence', then 'evil influence', such as an epidemic), *umbrella* (originally=sunshade), *confetti, spaghetti, dilettante, madonna,* and political terms such as *duce* and *fascist,* perhaps connected with Lat. *fasces,* a bundle of rods with an axe used as a symbol of authority in Roman times. A recent importation from Ital. is *espresso* (coffee and bar).

From the Scandinavian languages a few words have come in modern times: *ski, fiord, geyser, viking, valkyrie, sloyd, sko(a)l, smörgåsbord,* etc. From Russian we have *czar, duma, vodka, pogrom, tovarich, bolshevik(ism), soviet, ogpu, cheka,* and *sputnik.*

A number of Celtic words were taken into the language during the Mod. period, supplementing the few that were adopted in O.E. Examples are (from Scottish): *glen, pibroch, sporran, clan, cairn, plaid, whiskey* and the popular term *slogan* (originally=war-cry); *flannel, cromlech, gull* (a bird) possibly from Welsh; *bog, brogue, galore, shamrock, tory, colleen* from Irish. Note also *Dail* (pronounced *doil*), the name for the Irish Parliament.

From non-European languages there are the numerous words taken from the American Indians, first in North America, and then passing into English across the Atlantic, especially through "redskin" literature. Examples are *wigwam, tomahawk, squaw, moccasin, toboggan.* Other American words have remained primarily North American, e.g. *mugwump, squash,* etc.

Many other languages outside Europe have made their contributions to the vocabulary. From Hebrew we have a number of words: *amen, hallelujah, cherub*(*im*), *seraph*(*im*), *rabbi, sabbath, manna;* some of these, of course, are found in English before the Mod. period. From Yiddish, a mixture of Hebrew and German dialectal words, we have some expressions perhaps more common in the U.S.A. than in England: *ganof* (a thief), *goy* (a Christian), *kosher, mazuma* (slang=money).

There are numerous words of Arabic origin in English, though many of these have entered the language not directly from Arabic but through Fr. or some other language. A group of words beginning with *al–* (=*the* in Arabic) are of Arabic origin: *alcohol, alkali, algebra* (through Ital.), *alchemy* (through Fr.), *almanac* (through Spanish). In the word *admiral* (from Arabic through Fr.), the ending *–al* shows this same particle; it is derived from some such Arabic phrase as *amir-al-bahr* (Prince [of] the Sea); the *d* is a later insertion on the analogy of the common prefix *ad–*. There are also picturesque exotics such as *sheik, harem, houri, hookah, islam, koran, mufti, muezzin, fakir, ghoul, vizier.* More common words are *sofa* and *orange; sugar* and *candy* come from Arabic through Fr.

The Anglo-Indian has introduced a number of terms through his contact with the various languages of that continent. Thus we have *pukka* (a *pukka sahib*=a regular fellow), *chit*(*ty*), the British *raj* (rule), *rajah, bungalow, shampoo, chintz, jungle, loot, thug, pariah, dinghy, khaki, pundit,* etc., as well as a few slang expressions, such as *blighty* and *cushy,* current during World War I.

The Chinese and Japanese have not provided us with many words. A few examples of these Oriental contributions can be seen in names of dishes, *chop suey, chow mein*, games, *fan tan*, *mah jong*, and miscellaneous words like *kow-tow*, *rickshaw*, a shortening of *jinricksha*, *ju-jitsu*, *kimono*, *tycoon*, and the political term *kuomintang* for the Chinese nationalist movement. *Joss*, a god, probably from Port. *deos* (cf. Lat. *deus*) and *look-see*, a survey, are examples of "pidgin English".

This catalogue of foreign loans could be continued at great length, but enough have probably been given to indicate the variety of sources from which Mod. E. has built up its vocabulary.[4]

It is of interest to note the varying proportion of native and non-native words in the vocabulary of certain English authors. The results of an enquiry into this problem will differ considerably according to whether the calculation is based on a complete count of the words used by an author or an examination of selected passages. The first method provides what might be called a "static", the second a "dynamic", picture of the writer's vocabulary. The latter procedure is obviously closer to the real facts. The differences in the statistics arrived at by the two methods are often very large. We have already seen in M.E., that in Chaucer's writings, the complete count gives slightly over half, the "sampling" method less than twenty per cent of non-native words. Similarly, if a calculation is made of the modern vocabulary based on entries in a dictionary, the foreign element will turn out to be much greater than the native element, the proportion of borrowed words to native words being as high as three or four to one.[5] But

[4] For detailed discussion of these Mod. loan-words, besides L. P. Smith's book mentioned above, such works as H. Bradley, *The Making of English*, Greenough and Kittredge, *Words and Their Ways in English Speech*, G. H. McKnight, *English Words and Their Background*, O. Jespersen's *Growth and Structure of the English Language*, M. S. Serjeantson, *A History of Foreign Words in English*, should be consulted.

[5] O. F. Emerson, *A Brief History of the English Language*, p. 119.

in the actual writings of modern English authors the percentage of loan-words is far lower. Emerson (*loc. cit.*) has given some figures which are of interest. While three Gospels of the Bible show only six per cent of words of foreign origin, and Shakespeare has only ten per cent, Milton has nineteen, Johnson twenty-eight, and Gibbon thirty. These statistics are, however, based on a calculation which takes into account each word as often as it occurs; if each word were only counted a single time the percentage of non-native words would be considerably higher, as it is obvious that the native words occur with much greater frequency than the others. These figures are the result of investigation of selected passages; an examination of the total vocabulary gives forty per cent of Romance words alone in the language of the Bible and of Shakespeare, and 67 per cent in Milton's works. We may also note some statistics about the number of words used in these different works. While Chaucer makes use of slightly over 8,000 words, the vocabulary of the English Authorized Version has been calculated at 6,568 words, while estimates of Shakespeare's vocabulary range from 15,000 to 25,000, the low figure probably being closer to the truth, and Milton has been credited with from 8,000 to 13,000 words.[6] In our own day Churchill used probably 50,000 to 60,000.

The proportion of the two groups of words—native and foreign—changes in different parts of the same author's work, according to the nature of the subject matter, the emotional tone of the passage, and other factors which affect his choice of words. Some striking examples of this extreme range within the vocabulary of a single author have already been given in Chapter 2. Our language is an instrument which, in the hands of a skilled artist, is capable of infinite variety.

[6] J. Mersand, *Chaucer's Romance Vocabulary*, p. 52.

9. The Structure of Modern English

The transition from M.E. to Mod. E. is marked by a striking series of sound changes which are difficult to date with any great degree of exactness. Many of them are of so radical a nature that they must have been spread over a long period of time. Some appear late in the modern period, others early. The two revolutionary developments discussed at the beginning of this chapter, the loss of final vowels and the so-called "great vowel-shift", are among the earliest changes, probably going back to the late M.E. period, i.e. the fifteenth century, or making a sporadic appearance even before this date, according to the evidence of spellings adduced by scholars who have investigated this problem.[1] This suggestion of an earlier dating of the vowel shift is one reason for placing the end of the M.E. period and the beginning of Mod. E. some time before 1500, and 1450 is now often given as the boundary between the two stages of the language. We must remember, however, as has already been pointed out, that any such date is arbitrary, that the process of change was gradual and imperceptible, extending over many generations before it was finally accomplished and probably proceeding at a different pace in different parts of the country and different social levels. We have only to think of what is going on in our language today to realize that a uniform development obeying rigid rules could never have existed.

[1] See H. C. Wyld, A History of Modern Colloquial English and R. E. Zachrisson, The Pronunciation of English Vowels—1400–1700.

At any moment there must have been tendencies towards various types of change; sometimes, however, one tendency seems to get the upper hand and gradually to establish itself over a large region, thus causing the standard language to develop a new feature. The two processes mentioned above are so far-reaching in their effects on the structure of the language that by the time they are established we may say we are in the modern period. But just as we allow for a considerable interval during which the language was in a transition stage between O.E. and M.E., so there is an intermediate period of indefinite length between M.E. and Mod. E.

THE SOUNDS OF MOD. E.

The two outstanding changes in the vowel system as we pass from M.E. to Mod. E. have already been indicated. They are:

(1) The loss of many final vowels in unstressed syllables, especially the vowel *e*.

(2) Changes in the long vowels of stressed syllables, sometimes called "the great vowel-shift".

Because so many final vowels, which had already been weakened in M.E., vanished completely by the modern period, the three stages of the language, O.E., M.E. and Mod. E., are often called respectively the period of "full endings", the period of "reduced endings", and the period of "lost endings". This loss of final vowels may have begun in late M.E., but the process is complete by early Mod. E. The following examples illustrate these changes:

O.E.	M.E.	Mod. E.
cēp*an*	kep*ee*(*n*)	keep
heort*e*	hert*e*	heart

nam*a*	name (*e* still		name (*e* silent)	
	pronounced)			
luf*u* (noun)	love *"*	*"*	love *"*	*"*
luf*ian* (verb)	love(*n*) *"*	*"*	love *"*	*"*
wǽr*on*	were(*n*) *"*	*"*	were *"*	*"*
stān*as*	stoon*es* *"*	*"*	stones *"*	*"*

These various endings, all reduced to the neutral *e* in
M.E., have entirely disappeared in Mod. E., though the
e is often kept in the spelling. But it must be noted that
in Mod. E. *name, love,* etc. the last *sound* is a consonant,
m or *v.* One important result of this loss is that there is
often no longer any distinguishing mark between the form
of a noun and a verb. Thus the verb *lufian* and the noun
lufu are both levelled under *love.* In consequence it became very easy for a word to change from one part of
speech to another; a noun may be used as a verb or a verb
as a noun; even an adjective may function as a noun or
verb without any difference of external form. This is particularly frequent in Shakespearian English, which shows
in this respect a freedom that is parallel to modern American usage.[2] Here is an example taken at random from
Shakespeare (*King Lear*):

> my face I'll *grime* with filth;
> *Blanket* my loins; *elf* all my hair in knots.

In one sentence three nouns have been turned into verbs,
with a strikingly vivid effect.

Another result of the loss of final *e* is the levelling of
the adverb in *e* (see p. 68) with the corresponding adjective. Now M.E. *fast* (adj.) and *faste* (adv.), *long* and
longe coincide in form; we can thus say *a long road* (adj.)
or *it won't last long* (adv.); this accounts for a number of
new adverbs in *–ly*, e.g. *slowly*; apparently the "flat" ad-

[2] See p. 191.

verb *slow* did not have enough adverbial force, and so a second adverb is built up on the analogy of the *–ly* type. This tendency to extend the *–ly* ending may perhaps account for the curious North American idiom "to feel *badly* about something".

The so-called "great vowel shift" is difficult to explain in non-technical language and without the use of a phonetic alphabet. Stated in a somewhat simplified manner, it consists of a series of changes which affected the long vowels of M.E. and gradually transformed them into quite different sounds in Mod. E. It is the most revolutionary and far-reaching sound change during the history of the language and naturally took a long time to complete. It probably started in late M.E.

(1) M.E. ī (EE) AND ū (OO)

Let us start with O.E. and M.E. ī (pronounced like *ee* in *see*). This, like other long vowels, did not change between O.E. and M.E. Thus O.E. *bītan* is M.E. *bīte* with the same root vowel. But in Mod. E. this M.E. ī (*ee*) becomes the Mod. sound in *bite*, which is really not a single vowel at all but a diphthong composed of two vowels, first the sound *a* (about as in *father*) followed by the sound *i* (as in *bit*). This can be tested by the simple experiment of pronouncing these two vowels rapidly and allowing them to merge into one syllable. An exactly parallel process can be seen in the O.E. and M.E. ū sound. O.E. *hūs* (pronounced *hoos*) is unchanged in M.E., though it is spelt *hous*, but in Mod. E. this *oo* sound becomes the sound *ow* as in *now*; this is also a diphthong, made up of a sound *a* (as in *father*)+a sound *u* (as in *push*). This too can be tested by experiment. We have then O.E. and M.E. ī (*ee*) > Mod. E. "long *i*" and O.E. and M.E. ū (*oo*) > Mod. E. *ou* or *ow*. Here are some examples:

O.E.	mīn	þīn	rīdan	rīsan	tīd, etc.
M.E.	myn	thyn	ride(n)	rise(n)	tid
Mod.E.	mine	thine	ride	rise	tide

M.E. *i* or *y* pronounced *ee*.
Mod. E. "long" *i*=a+i.

O.E.	hūs	cū	þūsend	ābūtan
M.E.	hous	cou	thousand	aboute
Mod.E.	house	cow	thousand	about

O.E. mūð
M.E. mouth (*ou*=oo)
Mod.E. mouth (*ou*=a+u)

(2) M.E. Ē AND Ō

While M.E. ī and ū were changing in the way described above, two other M.E. sounds were taking their place in the Mod. sound-system. These were M.E. ē (pronounced about as in *say*) and M.E. ō (as in *go*), which became Mod. *ee* and *oo*. This second shift may be illustrated by the following examples:

O.E. fēt (pronounced *fate*)		tēð	mētan
M.E. feet	" "	teeth	me(e)te(n)
Mod.E. feet		teeth	meet

Another M.E. ē sound which had a slightly different pronunciation also became *ee* (often spelt *ea*) in Mod. E. Examples are:

O.E.	rǣdan	bēatan	lǣdan
M.E.	rede(n)	bete(n)	lede(n)
Mod.E.	read	beat	lead (verb)

Parallel to this change of M.E. *ē* to Mod. *ee* is the movement of M.E. *ō* to Mod. *oo*. Examples are:

O.E.	sōna	fōt	dōm	gōd
M.E.	sone (soone)	foot	doom	god(e)
	(*oo* pronounced *o*)			
Mod.E.	soon	foot	doom	good

It will be seen that this *oo* has not quite the same sound in *soon* and *foot* or *doom* and *good*.

(3) M.E. Ā AND "OPEN" Ō

Now that *ē* has become *ee* and *ō* has become *oo* two new *ē* and *ō* sounds develop. These are from M.E. *ā* (pronounced as in *father*) and "open" *o* (pronounced as in *saw*) respectively. Here are some examples:

O.E.	nama	taka (late O.E.)	hlæfdīge
M.E.	name	take	lady(e)
	(pronounced *nahmë*)		
Mod.E.	name (nēm)	take	lady

O.E.	āc	hām	stān
M.E.	ook (awk)	hoom (hawm)	stoon (stawn)
Mod.E.	oak	home	stone

O.E.	hopa
M.E.	hope (hawpë)
Mod.E.	hope

Of these words three, as we see, go back to O.E. *a*; *hope* has a different origin; it has a short *o* in O.E., which has been later lengthened.

The main features of the whole process can be seen in the accompanying diagrams.

SOUNDS

M.E.	*a* (as in M*a*)	*e* (M*a*e)	*i* (m*e*)
	↓	↓	↓
Mod.E.	ae (as in M*a*e)	ee (m*e*)	ie (m*y*)

M.E.	'open' *o* (d*aw*)	'close' *o* (d*o*e)	*u* (d*o*)
	↓	↓	↓
Mod.E.	œ (d*o*e)	oo (d*o*)	ou (d*ou*bt)

WORDS

M.E.	name (n*ah*më)	fet (fate)	min (m*ee*n)
	↓	↓	↓
Mod.E.	name	feet	mine

M.E.	boon (b*aw*n)	so(o)ne (soenë)	h(o)us (hoos)
	↓	↓	↓
Mod.E.	bone	soon	house

A number of words had their vowels shortened in the early Mod. period, especially before the sounds *d, t, f, th.* This explains the pronunciation of such words as *dead, bread, head* as compared with *read* (to read), and the usual British pronunciation of *eat* (past) as *et*, as well as *sweat, threat(en)*. Before *f* we have *deaf* with short *e*, though *deef* can still be heard in certain dialects; before *th* we have *death, breath.*

A third vowel-change which affected a large group of words and which is reflected in certain differences between British and North American English today is the change from M.E. *er* to Mod. E. *ar*. This may have started, like the dropping of final *e*, in late M.E. It can be seen by comparing a number of M.E. words found, for instance, in Chaucer, with the corresponding words in Mod. E.

Chaucer	*Mod. E.*
sterre	star
derke	dark
ferthing	farthing
herte	heart
sterve	starve
fer	far
werre	war

In *war* the Mod. vowel is different because of the influence of the *w*. This change of *er* to *ar* does not always show itself in Mod. E. In the early Mod. period the two types existed side by side; in some words the *er* type prevailed, in others the *ar* type. Thus we still have the *er* pronunciation in *learn*, *earth*, *certain*, etc., though in earlier times *larn*, *sartin*, etc. were common. In some words there is a double pronunciation, e.g. *clerk*, where many English speakers have *ar*, but North American English generally has *er*. *Derby* is pronounced both with *er* and *ar* by British speakers, *hearth* has *ar*, but *er* can be heard in dialectal speech, especially in North America. In *sergeant* we preserve the *er* spelling, but usually hear *ar*. In *person*, *parson* both forms have survived with a difference in meaning. Occasionally in North American rural dialects *varmint* for *vermin* can still be heard.

There are many other vowel-changes in the Mod. period, but those discussed above are perhaps the most radical and far-reaching in their effects on the language.

Consonant Changes

(A) LOSS OF CONSONANTS

Mod. E. sees the continued loss of consonants that had begun to show itself in M.E.; in some words, however, consonants are added. The main groups of words in which consonants are lost are as follows:

(1) Loss of initial *k*, *g*, *w* in the combinations *kn-*, *gn-*, *wr-*, etc. The simplification of these groups of sounds took place rather late in the history of the language. The *k* in words like *know, knight, knee* probably did not completely disappear until the eighteenth century, though its loss begins late in the seventeenth. The same is true of the *g* in *gnat, gnaw*, etc. Thus Shakespeare and Milton would have pronounced these letters. The *w* in *wrong, wry, wright*, etc., was lost about the same time or a little earlier.

(2) The loss of the *gh* sounds in *night, nought*, etc. took place early in the seventeenth century. Some words, however, instead of dropping the *gh* sound, changed it to *f*, though *gh* remains in the spelling: *enough, rough, cough, laugh*, etc.

(3) A final *b* is often lost in the combination *-mb*, probably in late M.E. One result of this development of a silent *b* is, as we shall see, that a *b* was sometimes wrongly added to a word which originally ended with *m*, e.g. *limb*, where the O.E. form was *lim*. In *comb, lamb*, etc. the *b* is genuine; in earlier English it was pronounced.

(4) Loss of *r*. In "Standard" English *r* has been lost when final or before another consonant, i.e. in words like *far, stir* and *hard, work*. This tendency showed itself sporadically a good deal earlier than the Mod. period, but became general in Mod. E. Outside Standard English and in North America various types of *r* sounds are still heard in these positions, ranging from the full consonant used by many Scottish speakers to the faint "*r*-colouring" of the preceding vowel retained in certain English and North American dialects. In the United States, however, especially in the South and the East, many speakers drop the *r* just as in Standard English.

(5) The *t* sound is frequently lost, especially between

two consonants, e.g. *castle, whistle, mistletoe, Christmas, postman*. Before *en* it is usually silent in *listen, hasten, soften,* etc.; in *often* it is restored by some speakers.

(6) A final *f* has been lost in a few words taken from Fr., e.g. *jolly*, where the earlier form is still retained in the name *Joliffe, hasty*, O. Fr. *hastif, tardy*, Fr. *tardif, testy*, O. Fr. *testif*. The same loss is seen in the Eng. word *hussy* from *hūswīf*.

(B) ADDITION OF CONSONANTS

In some words consonants have been added in Mod. E. A few examples are as follows:

(1) Addition of *d*.

A final *d* has been attached to words like *sound*; cf. M.E. *soun* (from Fr. *son, soun*). The same process is seen in *bound* as in "bound for a place", M.E. *boun*, and *expound*, M.E. *expoune*.

(2) Addition of *t*.

A final *t* is added to a few words such as *against, amongst*, M.E. *agens, amonges*. The reason for these additions is the attraction of a common verbal pattern in *–nd* and *–st*. We can see the same process at work today in the dialectal *oncet*, probably influenced by *first*, and *acrost*. A *t* is also added to words like *peasant* (cf. Fr. *paysan*), *tyrant* (Fr. *tyran*), etc. Here too a similar process can be detected in the dialectal *orphant, sermont*.

(3) Addition of *h*.

In many words of Fr. origin, which in M.E. appeared without an *h*, this sound has been restored in Mod. E., e.g. M.E. (*h*)*oost*, (*h*)*omage*, etc. Gradually in Mod. E. the *h* was sounded in this group of words except for *heir*(*ess*), *hour, honour*(*able*), etc. There is still some fluctuation, especially in North America, in such words as *herb, humble, human, humour*, but the *h* is probably on its way back. In (*h*)*ostler* both forms have survived.

(4) Insertion of *n*.

An *n* has been inserted in such words as *passenger, messenger, porringer* (cf. *passage, message, porridge*), *harbinger*, M.E. *herbergere*, 'one who provides shelter'. The change is due to analogy; the same tendency can be seen in the dialectal *sassengers* for *sausages*.

MOD. E. SPELLING

Until the M.E. period English had to some extent kept pace with pronunciation. With the invention of printing in the fifteenth century and the increasing influence of the written language, the lag between pronunciation and spelling tends to increase, so that in many respects our present spelling reflects the M.E. rather than the Mod. pronunciation. Thus letters like *gh* in *night*, *k* in *know*, *g* in *gnaw*, *e* in *have* are retained long after the sounds they formerly represented disappeared. A few changes were made in the spelling during the Renaissance period, some of which, as we shall see, were not improvements, and some in the eighteenth century, but no radical overhauling of English orthography has taken place during the Mod. period; as a result our spelling is defective in many directions.

Some of the changes in spelling during the age of the Renaissance (16th century) were not altogether happy. They were sometimes based on incorrect theories about the origin of English words and on attempts, often misguided, to bring English closer to Latin and Greek. Many "silent" letters were inserted in English words. Thus, for instance, the word *island* had previously been written *iland* or *yland*; this was correct, both phonetically and historically, as it is derived from O.E. *ī(g)land*. But later the word came to be associated, not unnaturally, with *isle*, and consequently the *s* was inserted into the spelling. Actually the words are not connected at all; the English word *isle* is borrowed from the older French *isle* (Mod. Fr. *île*), which goes back to Latin *insula; island* is a Teutonic word that never had an *s* sound at any time in its history.

In other words silent letters were added with slightly more justification. The *b* was inserted in *doubt* and *debt* to suggest the connection with Lat. *dubito* and *debitum*, whereas actually these words were not borrowed directly from Lat. but came in through Fr., where the *b* had already disappeared; cf. Fr. *doute, dette.* Thus Chaucer's spelling *doute* and *dette* are more historical and more phonetic than our own.

The spelling *rhyme* is due to the same tendency. Like *debt* and *doubt* it was a loan-word from Fr., taken over in the form *rime* or *ryme*; in the sixteenth century the spelling was changed to *rhyme* to suggest a connection with *rhythm*. In recent times, however, there is a movement back to the earlier form *rime*.

The *ch* in *school* (*scholar*) is another attempt to give a word a more classical appearance. An early loan from Lat., it is found as *scol* in O.E. Chaucer has *scol(e)*; the *h* was inserted to bring it in line with Lat. *schola*.

The much-debated *schedule* is somewhat similar. Here the M.E. form was *cedule* or *sedule*, from O. Fr. *cedule*. But, because this Fr. word was connected with the Mediaeval Lat. *schedula*, the spelling was changed so as to show this. We ought thus to say *sedule* in Mod. E.; historically neither *sk–* nor *sh–* is correct. In *schism*, M.E. *cisme*, exactly the same thing has happened, but in this case the pronunciation has remained unchanged (*sizm*) in spite of the "learned" spelling with *sch–*.

Other attempts to "reform" the spelling can be seen in the new form *delight* for M.E. *delit*, the *gh* inserted on the analogy of *night, right*, etc., the addition of *h* to *ghost, ghastly, aghast*, from O.E. *gāst*, M.E. *go(o)st*, etc., and the prefixing of *w* to *whole*, O.E. *hāl*, M.E. *ho(o)l*. After *b* had been lost in words with final *–mb* an unhistorical *b* was added in the spelling in several cases, e.g. *limb*, O.E. *lim*, *thumb*, O.E. *ðūma*, etc. On the analogy of *would* and *should*, M.E. *wolde* and *sholde*, a silent *l* was inserted in *could*; this is not justified historically, as the M.E. form was *coude*, O.E. *cūðe*, past tense of *can*. At one time there was even an attempt to pronounce this *l*.

In the Mod. period there is a good deal of fluctuation in the spelling of the ending *–or* as in *hono(u)r*, *terror*, etc. In the eighteenth century many words which today are spelt with *–or* had *–our*, e.g. *errour*, *authour*. Gradually, however, the distinction between *–or* and *–our* words was established; it is not, as far as can be seen, based on any very definite historical principle, and on the American continent the *–or* spelling has been much more widely adopted than in England, e.g. *honor*, *labor*, etc. A similar uncertainty shows itself in the eighteenth century about the ending *–io*, when we often find *–ick* where today we have *–ic*, e.g. *comick*, *publick*, probably on the analogy of *thick*, *sick*, etc. But the *k* was dropped later in this ending.

MOD. E. FORMS

The process of reduction of endings and levelling of forms had already proceeded very far by the end of the M.E. period; in Mod. E. they become what we are familiar with today.

The Noun

The plural and possessive forms of the noun generally drop the vowel of the ending, i.e. M.E. *stoones*, pronounced in two syllables, loses the sound of the *e*. In *fishes*, *judges*, etc., this sound is preserved. The plural in *s* gains ground at the expense of the unchanged plural and the *–en* plural.

The Adjective

The last vestige of the inflection of the adjective, the final *e* (see p. 92) disappears in Mod. E. The comparative and superlative become regularly *-er* and *-est* (or *more, most*) without any change of the root vowel except in *old, elder, eldest*, which are found by the side of the regular forms *older, oldest*.

The Adverb

The ending *-ly* is added to a number of adverbs which in M.E. had *-e*, and therefore should normally have had in late M.E. and Mod. E. the same form as the adjective, as in *fast, long*. This accounts for new forms such as *slowly* by the side of the adverb *slow*; the adverbial use of *slow* is still seen clearly in such a line as Shakespeare's: How *slow* this old moon wanes.

The Verb

The two forms of the past tense that were frequently found in the strong verbs in M.E.—*I sang, we sungen, I rood, we riden*—are levelled in Mod. E. As a result the past tense, weak or strong, shows no variety in its paradigm in Mod. E. (*loved, sang* are both unchanged). The prefix of the past participle, *y-*, still occasionally found in M.E., has disappeared entirely in Mod. E., except for a few fossil forms. The *-en* of the past participle appears in certain strong verbs but not in others; compare *written, chosen, eaten, shaken* with *sung, drunk*. In some cases two forms have survived, e.g. *drunk* and *drunken*, with specialized uses in Mod. E. The retention of this ending seems largely a matter of accident; thus, we have *forgotten* by the side of *got*, though in North American English a participle *gotten* is also heard. In earlier Mod. E. past participles such as *spoke, wrote*, etc., are not uncommon; today they belong to uneducated speech.

Early Mod. E. still shows the verb endings *–est, –eth*; later they are lost except in biblical and poetical language. This leaves only one inflection *–s–* for the present tense.

Pronouns

The most revolutionary development in the Mod. pronoun is the complete disappearance of any difference between the singular and the plural of the second personal pronoun; *ye* and *you, thou* and *thee* are all levelled under the one form *you; thy, thine* and *your* under *your(s)*. One consequence of this is that there is no longer any way of indicating by a pronoun whether one is addressing a single person or a number of people. This difficulty explains uneducated and dialectal formations such as *you-all, youse* in order to suggest the idea of plurality. Another result is that, unlike many other languages, English does not make a distinction between formal and informal address by means of a change of pronoun; we use *you* all the time, unlike, for instance, Fr. and Ger., which change the formal *vous, Sie* to the informal *tu, du*. This occasionally causes a difficulty in translating from these languages, where the shift in the pronoun may indicate a significant change in the relationship between two people—the French have a name for it: *tutoyer*. But the universal use of *you* as a form of address is probably on the whole an advantage; the "double standard" of the pronoun in other languages is sometimes embarrassing socially; one is not quite certain whether to use the formal or the more familiar one; no such problem can arise in English.

The new possessive pronoun *its* originates in the Mod. period.

MOD. E. SYNTAX

The syntax of Mod. E. is a vast subject of which only a few features can be discussed here. Some characteristics have already been pointed out in Chapter 1: the development of an elaborate system of tenses in the verb, the disappearance, in educated speech, of the double negative, the almost complete loss of the subjunctive—these are only a few out of the hundreds of interesting syntactical items in the Mod. E. picture.[3]

While there are some traces of our complex tense system in the O.E. and M.E. verb, we have to wait till Mod. E. for its full blossoming and the specialization of the different forms, e.g. the exact shades of meaning in *I write, I am writing, I do write*; in fact some of our verbal constructions have appeared in the language quite recently. A case in point is seen in a phrase like *the house is being built*. Not long ago this construction was bitterly attacked by some grammarians as an innovation, a disgrace to the English language; its opponents defended the older idiom *the house is building*. We need not go far back to find books on "correct English", talking about "the house is being built" in the same way as some writers attack the "split infinitive" today, and it is possible that this construction (e.g. *to quickly act*) may in the course of time become recognized without any disastrous effect on the language. As in vocabulary, so in syntax, it is dangerous to prophesy and to say that a certain form of speech will or will not be ultimately accepted.

The verb forms used in negative and interrogative sentences become established in Mod. E. and displace the older constructions. Thus *He knows not* and *Know you*

[3] For a detailed account of Eng. syntax see Jespersen, *A Modern English Grammar*, vols. 2 and 3 and Curme, *A Grammar of the English Language*, vol. 3.

(or *ye*)? give way to *He does not know* and *Do you know?*, except in archaic or poetic language, where the older forms may survive. The complex rules about the use of *shall* and *will*, *should* and *would*, more faithfully observed in British ("Standard") than in North American English, are a product of the Mod. period.

Mod. E. sees the specialization of the relative pronouns, *who, which* and *that*. Even in early Mod. E. their use is not so uniform as today, as *which* is still frequently found referring to persons. This usage is common, for instance, in biblical English, e.g. *Our father, which art in heaven*, or *The Amorites which dwelt in the land*. Gradually, however, during the modern period, *which* is restricted in its use, until now it refers only to inanimate objects, *who* and *that* being used for people.

There is a tendency, perhaps increasing, to avoid *whom*, especially in colloquial speech. Thus, although it is incorrect from the point of view of formal grammar, *Who are you going with?* is a more normal Mod. idiom than the more correct *With whom are you going?* Again it is dangerous to prophesy, but one feels that *whom* may become in time a linguistic fossil. The people who still use it may come to be classed with those who insist on *It's I*.

Just as double negatives were common until quite recently, so a double comparative or superlative was frequently used in the adjective and, like the repeated negative, still persists in uneducated speech. Thus we have Shakespeare's well-known line: "This was the *most* unkind*est* cut of all" (*Julius Caesar*), where the duplication of *most* and *–est* is probably intended for emphasis. In the same century we find "*the most diligentest bishop*". Even as late as Tennyson, we have "*more lovelier than all the world*", though this is probably an intentional "poetic licence". Shakespeare also uses forms such as *worser, more kinder*, a double comparative not unknown today. We might note here, though it comes more strictly under the heading of forms, that the rule about adding *more* and *most* to indicate comparison in adjectives of several syllables is fairly recent. The form *diligentest* has already been quoted, and Shakespeare has words such as *ancienter*, *violentest*, where we should say *more ancient, most violent*.

A curious syntactical feature of late M.E. and early Mod. E. is the expansion of the possessive ending *–s* into a pronoun *his*, chiefly after names of persons. This was apparently due to a mistaken idea that the *–s* was originally a contraction of *his*, a theory which is quite unfounded. The seventeenth century Prayer Book has *for Jesus Christ* his *sake*, in the eighteenth century we find *King Edward the Fourth* his *death*; in both phrases we should use the ending *–s* today. This construction was occasionally extended even to the feminine and plural, e.g. *Juno* hir *bedde* (=Juno's bed), *Canterberry and Chillingworth*, their *books*.[4] A striking example of the flexibility of Mod. E. is seen in the way in which the possessive *–s* can be attached to a long phrase, e.g. *the Under-secretary of State's speech, the Knight of the Round Table's armour*; these informal constructions would be difficult to find in most other languages. Another possibility in Mod. E. which cannot be easily paralleled in other languages is the use of a complex phrase as an adjective, e.g. *with a hit-me-if-you-dare expression on his face*.

A feature of Mod. syntax which seems to be spreading, probably because of the influence of the Press, is the habit of combining two nouns into a phrase and omitting a preposition which would formerly have been used to connect them. Thus instead of *an attempt at murder* we read of *a murder attempt, a trial for murder* is *a murder trial, a robbery of a bank* is *a bank robbery, shooting on the frontier* is *frontier shooting*, and so on.

[4] Quoted by H. C. Wyld, *A History of Modern Colloquial English.*

10. Changes in Meaning

So far we have been considering the various changes that have taken place in the form and arrangement of English words and the new material that has been added to the language by borrowing from outside. We must now examine a different kind of change in the language, by which a word is modified not merely in its outer form but in the meaning it conveys. The study of meaning, sometimes called Semantics, has received much attention recently because of the light that it throws on other subjects connected with language, especially logic and psychology. Certain writers, however, are now using the term Semantics in a broader sense which is no longer purely linguistic.

Some well-known examples of change in meaning have already been given in Chapter 1, and it is not difficult to detect these same processes at work today. A change seems to be taking place, for instance, in the word *maestro*, an Italian loan discussed in Chapter 8. Originally this term was applied to a great composer, teacher or conductor of music; then it was applied loosely to any great artist; then, half-humorously, to any artist at all; and finally, one can hear it attached to almost any performer in any field: radio announcers talk about "a hockey maestro", "a skating maestro", etc. The word *maestro* seems to be destined for the same fate as *professor*. This illustrates one very common type of semantic change, in which a word expands its range of meaning and is applied to situations where, formerly, it would have been inappropriate. It may be called *Widening of Meaning*. It is perhaps not so common as the opposite tendency, i.e., for a word to have its range of meaning restricted or narrowed, so that it covers only a portion of the ideas or objects it previously denoted. A good example of this is seen in Chapter 1, where we found that the word *deer*, which, as late as Shakespeare's age could be used in the wide sense of *animal*,[1] is now restricted to mean one species of animal. Formerly it could be applied to such creatures as the lamb or the camel. This may be called *Narrowing of Meaning*.

Another very common semantic process was seen in the change of the word *hūswíf* (housewife) to *hussy*.[2] Here we observe a word used originally in a good sense gradually taking on a very uncomplimentary meaning, on account of certain unpleasant associations that had come to be attached to it. This may be called *Lowering of Meaning*. Finally, exactly the opposite may happen; a word that at one time had a bad meaning may improve and lose its unpleasant associations, until it finishes by conveying a neutral or even a pleasing idea. An example of this is the word *fond*, which, as we shall see, originally meant *foolish*. This may be called *Raising of Meaning*. These are the four main semantic processes; to them may be added *Weakening* or *Fading of Meaning*, which is related both to the widening and raising processes.

NARROWING OF MEANING

Many examples can be found in all languages of words whose range of meaning has become narrower. A process parallel to that which affected *deer* shows itself in the word *meat*. At first this meant food of any kind, a usage

[1] The change from a general to a specific meaning had taken place, however, before Shakespeare's age; the Shakespearian phrase "mice and rats and such small deer" is an echo of earlier usage. See H. Bradley, *The Making of English*, p. 201.

[2] See p. 90.

that still survives in modern expressions such as *meat and drink, sweetmeats,* and that can be seen quite clearly in the M.E. extract given on p. 83 when Chaucer says of the Prioress:

> Ful semely after hir *mete* she raughte
> (She reached very politely for her *food*).

As meat was one very important article of diet the word gradually came to indicate this staple food, replacing the older word *flesh,* which can also be seen in Chaucer's description of the Prioress, when he tells us that she fed her dogs on "rosted flessh". *Flesh* itself, by a similar process of restriction, takes on as its main signification the flesh of human beings. It is interesting to note that exactly the same change took place in the Fr. word for meat, *viande,* which also originally meant food in general, as its Eng. form *viands* still does. This extract also provides us with another example, the word *houndes.* When Chaucer writes: "Of smale *houndes* hadde she . . ." he is not using *hounds* in the restricted sense generally applied to the word today, i.e. dogs for hunting, but in the general sense of *dogs.* The cognate Ger. *Hund* still retains the wider meaning.

Another instance is the word *wife.* This originally meant any woman and still does in the cognate Ger. *Weib,* and in English compounds such as *fishwife.* In earlier English we can see the wider range of meaning in Chaucer's *Wife of Bath,* which probably means simply the woman from Bath, although with her succession of five husbands she had certainly qualified for the more restricted title. The word *parson* illustrates the same tendency; originally the same word as *person,* it was restricted or specialized to mean one particular kind of person, a functionary of the church, and so we get the present difference between *person* and *parson.* This differentiation may have begun in Fr., from which the word is borrowed in M.E., or even in mediaeval Latin. An interesting contrast between the modern restricted meaning of a word and its wider Elizabethan sense can be seen in the term *undertaker*. Formerly this word meant one who undertook any enterprise (cf. Fr. *entrepreneur*, Ger. *Unternehmer*), especially one who undertook something on behalf of some other person. Now it is limited to what in North America is sometimes called a funeral director or mortician, i.e., a person who undertakes to bury people. The older meaning appears clearly in *Twelfth Night*, when Antonio offers to act on behalf of Viola in a quarrel, and Sir Toby says to him: "Nay, if you be an *undertaker*, I am (ready) for you", and draws his sword in preparation for a fight (*T.N.* III, 4, 320).

Some words have a wider range of meaning in England than in North America, e.g. *corn*, applied in England to all cereals, wheat, barley, oats, maize, etc., but in North America generally restricted to one variety, maize, probably an abbreviation of *Indian Corn*. On the other hand, such words as *shoe, bug, sick* are narrower in their meaning in England than in North America.[3]

Many other examples of this very common change can be found.

WIDENING OF MEANING

There seem to be fewer cases of widening than narrowing of meaning. To the example already given we may add one or two more. The word *place* formerly meant an open square in a town such as the *market place*, and is still frequently used in that sense in Fr.—*La Grande Place, Place de la Concorde*. From this it was extended to mean any place, and thus develops its wider modern

[3] See p. 190.

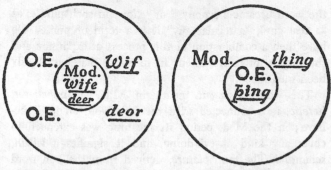

NARROWING OF MEANING.　　WIDENING OF MEANING.

meaning. The word *thing* is perhaps the term with the most vague and indefinite meaning in the whole English vocabulary. This was not always so; formerly it had a far narrower range of meaning. Thus in O.E. it meant *an assembly*, especially a court of law. In Iceland it is still used in this sense; the parliament of that country is called the *Althing*; the Norwegian parliament is the *Storting*, and the Danish lower chamber, the *Folketing*. It also came to mean in O.E. and M.E. a case brought before a court and then an *action, saying, idea*. Gradually it ceased to be mainly abstract, was extended to include concrete objects, and so in time took on its present-day wide meaning. In the realm of slang we have a good example of this widening of meaning in the fate of the word *guy*. This word originated from the first name of Guy Fawkes, one of the conspirators in the Gunpowder Plot to blow up the Houses of Parliament in 1605. Since this event, it has been the custom to burn an effigy of Guy Fawkes on November 5th, the anniversary of his abortive plot. As these effigies were usually fantastic in appearance, the word *guy* came to mean a stupid, grotesque person. This is one stage in the widening process. Then in North America the restricting idea of stupid or grotesque faded out, and the word became a synonym of *fellow*; in such phrases as "a real guy", "a regular guy" it is a term of praise. We have then a combination of this process of expansion and the process of improvement in meaning that has already been mentioned.

The word *miscreant* meant in M.E. an *unbeliever, heretic*; it is connected with the Lat. word *credo*, 'I believe'; in the Mod. period its meaning was extended to cover any kind of evil-doing, and it signifies a *villain, scoundrel*. The term *picture*, derived from the Lat. word meaning *to paint*, had originally the narrower signification of a painting but now covers a wider field—a photograph, for instance, can be referred to as a picture—and has widened its range by being used to describe "moving pictures". The North American use of the word *alibi* in the sense of *excuse* shows us this process of expansion at work. It is the Lat. word *alibi* 'elsewhere', used as one type of defence in a legal action, namely that a person was elsewhere when a crime was committed. But now in popular speech it is generalized to mean any kind of defence or excuse; *the team had no alibis to offer for its defeat* would be meaningless if *alibi* were being used in its restricted and legal sense.

Widening and narrowing of meaning sometimes appear in the same word. The two literary terms *lyric* and *ballad* illustrate this. A *lyric* was originally a song sung to the accompaniment of the *lyre*; then the term was used later to denote a certain type of non-narrative poetry (widening); today it is again being used to denote a song, especially as a semi-technical theatrical term (narrowing). *Ballad*, connected with a word meaning *to dance*, signified at first a poem or song used to accompany a dance, then a light sentimental song, a sense in which it is sometimes still used (widening), and later, a spirited and often tragic narrative poem in short stanzas (narrowing). A similar mixture of tendencies is present in the history of the word *cafeteria*. Derived from the Sp. word meaning a coffee-pot (Sp. *cafetera*), the name seems to have been transferred to the place where coffee was drunk (widening), then to any restaurant (widening), then finally to a restaurant with self-service (narrowing).

Under the heading of *Widening of Meaning*, we may consider cases where a concrete word has taken on an abstract meaning. A curious example is the word *chagrin*, of Fr. origin, originally meaning *rough skin*, and so giving the name to a rough kind of leather or skin which we now usually spell *shagreen*. But it came to be used also in a transferred metaphorical sense as *ill-humour*, *fretfulness*, etc., and so developed the present signification of chagrin, 'disappointment, mortification'. The word *humour*, which has a very interesting history and throws light on the mediaeval theory of medicine, is another example of the change from concrete to abstract, as well as a later restriction in meaning. In mediaeval medicine it meant one of the four fluids that the body was supposed to contain; then, as people were thought to possess certain qualities according to the proportion of these fluids, it came to mean about the same thing as *disposition, temperament*, thus passing from the concrete to an abstract term. Later, by a process of specialization, it was frequently used to denote the faculty of seeing and creating what is amusing, and so it develops its most ordinary modern sense, though it is still used in the wider sense as well, e.g., *to be in a bad (good) humour*.

Occasionally the opposite tendency is seen; words, formerly abstract, take on a concrete meaning. We have had one example in the word *thing*. Another can be observed in the treatment of the word *home* in North America, where, instead of remaining purely abstract, it is often used in the concrete sense of *house*, e.g., Beautiful *Homes* for Sale; Easy Terms. We even read of "machine-made homes" and "prefabricated homes". Another interesting case of a word taking on a more concrete signification is the adjective *buxom,* now referring to physical characteristics, formerly meaning *yielding, meek, gracious.*

A special case of expansion of meaning is seen in what might be called the weakening or fading of the idea behind a word; a term seems to lose its original force in the course of time. This is also closely related to the process of improvement in meaning. Several words, which at one time conveyed the idea of *immediately,* have been weakened and come to mean "in a little while"; it has been suggested that this reflects a strong human tendency to procrastinate. The two expressions *presently* and *by and by,* both of which now mean *shortly,* formerly meant "at once", as can be seen in many passages in Shakespeare. In the balcony scene in *Romeo and Juliet,* when Juliet is being called in by the Nurse and she replies *By and by, I come,* it is obvious that she means *immediately,* as she leaves Romeo almost at once (*R. and J.* II, 2, 151). The use of *presently* to suggest immediacy is reflected in a passage in *Macbeth* dealing with the King's healing touch, where the Doctor says (IV, 3, 143):

here at his touch,
Such sanctity hath heaven given his hand
They *presently* amend. (=they get better *at once*).

In the same way *present* is used in the sense of *immediate* in *R. and J.* V, 1, 50:

An if a man did need a poison now,
Whose sale is *present* death in Mantua,
Here lives a caitiff wretch would sell it him.

The word *presently* is now often used with the sense "at present" or "now," especially in North America.

Another example of this weakening process can be observed in the word *mere*, used frequently in earlier English in the sense *pure* or *complete, absolute*; its original meaning in Latin was *pure, unmixed*, generally applied to wine. In the scene already referred to in *Macbeth* (IV, 3, 150), Malcolm speaks of

> strangely-visited people,
> All swoln and ulcerous, pitiful to the eye,
> The *mere* despair of surgery, he cures,

where we should say "the *absolute* despair".

The colloquial language shows many instances of "fading". The adjectives *grand, wonderful* or *awful, terrible* are frequently used as labels which merely register approval or disapproval and no longer carry their original significance. The change of *naughty* from its older sense of *wicked* (see below) may also be considered as an example of this process.

LOWERING OF MEANING

A very common semantic phenomenon is the process by which a word comes to mean something worse than what it originally denoted. Like the tendency to procrastinate mentioned above, this too, is perhaps a reflection on human nature; certainly the words that have improved in meaning seem to be far fewer than those that have degenerated. This may be due to a general tendency to stress unpleasant rather than pleasant associations. On the other hand it may be quite natural that unpleasant associations cling to the mind more strongly than neutral or pleasant ones, and so tend to colour the meaning of a word. The word *hussy* has already been given as an illustration of this process, and to this we may add other nouns such as *knave*, which is derived from O.E. *knafa*, a boy. The Ger.

cognate *Knabe* still means *boy*. But as a boy is frequently up to mischievous pranks and sometimes may behave dishonourably, the bad meaning associated with the modern *knave* gradually developed. *Churl*, O.E. *ceorl*, a labourer, and *villain*, connected with *villein*, a term applied to one of the classes of serfs in the Middle Ages, *boor* (originally=*peasant*) show how opprobrious meanings come to be attached to the names of people who occupy a humble position in the social scale.

Adjectives also show this same change. The North American use of the word *homely* in the sense of "plain, ugly" is an obvious example. *Wanton* originally meant merely "unrestrained, sportive"; *lewd* has fallen seriously in the scale of meaning, starting as a word indicating the laity as opposed to the clergy, then meaning "unlearned, ignorant" because in the Middle Ages the layman was often ignorant, and finally developing its present morally reprehensible sense. *Silly* shows a similar history, though it has not sunk so low. In O.E. *sǽlig*, from which it is derived, meant *blessed, happy* (cf. Mod. Ger. *selig*, which is cognate); it then took on the meaning *simple*, and, later, just like one development of *simple* itself, degenerated into its modern sense.

We can see the same process at work in verbs. O.E. *stincan*, from which our word *stink* is derived, meant to give forth any kind of odour, good or bad; not infrequently it meant to smell sweetly. The same is true of the noun *stench*. Now both these words have taken on unpleasant associations. Today *smell* seems to be moving in the same direction; many people replace it by *odour*, which in its turn seems to be taking on an unpleasant meaning and may later be replaced by another word.

This substitution of *smell* for *stink* and *odour* for *smell* illustrates a linguistic process that is closely connected with degeneration of meaning. It is called *euphemism*, i.e., the use of a milder word instead of one that sounds too crude or harsh. It is a cumulative tendency; after a time the new expression itself often takes on the associations of the old one which it replaced, and it too has to be discarded. Euphemism is not a modern phenomenon; just as some people today avoid the words *die, death, dead*, preferring "to pass away", "passing", etc., so in O.E. words such as *gefaran*, "to depart", *forðferan*, "to journey", are commonly used. Even the idea of old age seems to be slightly improper; elderly people are *senior citizens*, an old age pension is a *retirement allowance*, and what used to be called the old folks home is now Sunset Manor. This dislike of certain expressions has its roots far back in the life of primitive man and is prevalent today among savages in the form of taboo. Nowadays we hear elderly ladies who refer to a *leg* as a *limb*, who *retire* instead of *going to bed*, the word *bed* apparently not being considered quite proper, and who call the *abdomen* the *lower chest*. The same motive changes *dirty clothes* into *soiled linen*. In the Victorian age the word *trousers* was considered not quite polite and was sometimes replaced by would-be-humorous terms like *unmentionables, inexpressibles, nether garments*. In rural districts today male animals are sometimes indicated by euphemistic substitutes; instead of *bull* one can hear the *animal*, the *critter*, the *big fellow*, the *he*, the *toro*, and even the *gentleman* (*cow*). This tendency is, however, not so much in evidence today as a generation or two ago; some would say that many speakers and writers are moving too far in the opposite direction and that there are too few inhibitions in the modern language of youth. After the *cause célèbre* of *Lady Chatterly's Lover* in England the four-letter word denoting the act of copulation, previously regarded as the most obscene term in our vocabulary, has received almost legal sanction and may in the future be used in circles where it was formerly taboo.

In contrast to the many words whose meaning has degenerated, we find a few with an improved sense. The best-known examples are *fond, nice, naughty*, all of which can be found in Shakespeare with meanings different from those they carry today. Thus *fond* meant *foolish*, as can be seen in *Romeo and Juliet*:

> Thou *fond* mad man, hear me a little speak.

Nice, which originally had the meaning *ignorant* (Lat. *nescius*), is used in Elizabethan English in the sense *foolish, trifling*; in our modern phrase "a nice point" we are still close to the sense *trifling*. *Naughty*, which is a mild term of reproach today, was much stronger in Shakespeare's age and is equivalent to Mod. *wicked*. Cf. *Merch. of Ven.* (V, 1, 91):

> So shines a good deed in a *naughty* world.

Another quotation from the same play illustrates this and also the word *fond*='foolish'. Shylock is upbraiding the gaoler for having allowed Antonio to come out of his prison (*Merch. of Ven.*, III, 3, 8):

> I do wonder,
> Thou *naughty* gaoler, that thou art so *fond*
> To come abroad with him at his request.

If we are to read Shakespeare or any other earlier writer intelligently it is clear that we have to be continually on our guard for the possibility of semantic change; we must be careful not to read into his words meanings which belong not to his day but to our own, and which he did not intend to convey. When we consider how much misunderstanding arises at the present time on account of inexact use of terms in writing and discussion, we can easily realize how much greater this danger is when we are dealing with utterances belonging to the past.

11. Levels in Language; the Rise of Informal Language

In Chapter 10 we discussed the raising or lowering of the meaning of words. We now pass to a somewhat similar question which might be described as the raising or lowering of the *status* of a word in the language. This does not necessarily involve any change of meaning, though sometimes the two processes go together, but often a word may keep its original signification, and, in the course of time, improve its standing or lose caste as a means of expression. Just as people rise and fall in the social scale, so words become more or less generally acceptable. This brings us to a consideration of what may be called levels in the language, an important problem for all who are concerned with writing. The three linguistic levels usually distinguished are (1) literary (2) colloquial and (3) slang. These are not clear-cut divisions, but, as we shall see, overlap considerably. It would be incorrect to think of the vocabulary of a language as three strata, one imposed on top of the other; the situation is not so simple as that shown in Fig. 1.

A more accurate idea would be given by a number of overlapping circles, (Fig. 2) showing a large region com-

FIG. 1.

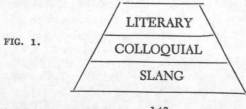

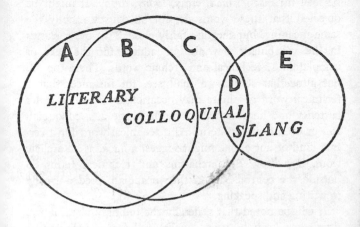

FIG. 2.

mon to the literary and colloquial language (B in the diagram) and another region (D) shared by colloquialisms and slang. This gives us five categories: (A) purely literary words and expressions; (B) expressions suitable either for literary or colloquial use; (C) purely colloquial expressions; (D) expressions on the border-line between colloquialisms and slang; (E) purely slang expressions.[1] It is not always easy to assign a given word to its exact position in this scheme; regions C and D especially are somewhat vague, but it is interesting to take a common idea or object and try to indicate it by means of words on these five different levels. Thus for the word horse one might suggest: A-*steed*; B-*horse*; C-*mount*; D-*dobbin*; E-*nag*. Or the state of intoxication might be described by A-*inebriated*; B-*drunk*; C-*merry* or *three sheets in the wind*; D-*tipsy*; E-*plastered* or *blotto*. A similar series can

---

[1] I am indebted for the idea of this diagram to C. C. Fries, *The Teaching of English*, p. 10, though my classification is somewhat different from his.

be seen in: *insane, mad, crazy, loony, dippy*. It might be objected that these words do not all convey exactly the same meaning, but they are fairly close. Two other classes in the vocabulary may also be added, for the sake of completeness: technical and archaic words. These too are not altogether stable; we shall see, for instance, that a technical word or phrase may occasionally obtain a wider currency and be accepted by the language as a colloquialism or even a literary term. As a technical word for a certain kind of horse, one might suggest a *hack*, as an archaic word, a *palfrey*. But archaisms and technical terms lie outside the central part of the vocabulary used normally in writing and speaking.

It will be noted that generally the ordinary word, *horse, drunk*, etc., can be used equally well for everyday colloquial purposes or for literature. We can say: He came home *drunk* last night (*Coll.*), or The tyrant was *drunk* with power (*Lit.*). It may perhaps be argued that we are not really using the same word in these two sentences; the outer form is identical, but the change from a literal to a metaphorical meaning gives us two separate items in our vocabulary.

Words do not always remain in the category in which they first appear. Sometimes they improve their standing; beginning as slang, they become acceptable as colloquialisms or even for literary purposes. Sometimes they descend from the literary into the slang region. The latter process is often connected with the development of euphemistic expressions, a phenomenon dealt with in the previous chapter. An example of a word whose standing has improved is *mob*. This was originally a shortened form of *mobile*, itself an abbreviation of Lat. *mobile vulgus*, 'the excitable crowd'; such shortenings are, as we shall see, a common method by which slang forms are created. It was at first strongly condemned, just as modern forms like *Prof.* and *Doc.*, for *Professor* and *Doctor*, meet with disapproval. Thus Swift in the *Tatler* (1710) criticizes this word and other informal terms that were fashionable at the time, such as *banter, bamboozle, kidney* ("a person of that *kidney*"), *bubble, bully,* all of which are acceptable today. He also objects to more learned coinages such as *speculation, operation, ambassador, preliminaries, communication,* another illustration of the danger of pronouncing judgment on innovations in language. Nowadays *mob* has long ceased to be felt as slang, and has improved its standing to such an extent that it may be used quite appropriately in a literary context, e.g. "a seething *mob* of rioters". Its place in the diagram is Section B. There would be no serious objection to the literary use of *banter* today, while *bamboozle*, though scarcely suitable for strictly literary purposes (except, of course, in dialogue), is at least a recognized colloquialism. All these and many other words have thus risen from level E to C or B in our diagram.

The opposite process can be seen in such a word as *blooming*, which declined during the nineteenth century from level A or B to E. In 1774 a poet could write about "his *blooming* bride"; even as late as Tennyson we find it can still be used as a serious adjective: "her *blooming* mantle torn".[2] Later, however, its status deteriorated, largely because it was used as a mild substitute for *bloody* —a euphemistic substitution—and soon it became a slang word. Like many earlier examples of slang, it is now out of date and may in time even regain its former position and meaning. The word *nymph*, previously a common poetical synonym for *girl, maiden*, especially in the eighteenth century, has gone completely out of fashion through too frequent use and scarcely produces any poetical effect to-

[2] Cf. Marvell's couplet: Near to this gloomy cloister's gates
  There dwelt the *blooming virgin* Thwaites.

day. A favourite eighteenth-century phrase, *the blooming nymph,* is quite spoiled for the modern critical reader, for whom these two words carry entirely different connotations from those prevalent in that age or earlier. Other examples of words that have fallen from grace can easily be found.

As slang is an important source from which new words are added to the vocabulary, and as a slang phrase may occasionally find its way to the higher regions of the language, it is necessary to define this term and to examine some of the methods by which slang originates. The exact origin of the word *slang* is not certain and it has been used with different meanings at different times, but, as employed today, it may be defined as unorthodox, informal use of language, generally with a humorous or would-be-humorous intention. It indicates a revolt against the restrictions of formal writing and speaking, a desire for novelty, and is therefore found mainly among the young, before their speech has settled down into more conventional patterns, though, as we shall see, slang itself often becomes stereotyped.

The creation of slang is by no means a new, purely modern phenomenon; it can be traced far back into the past. There are words in the classical languages that are exact parallels to some of our modern slang expressions. Thus in Latin the word *recalcitro,* which gives us our learned-looking *recalcitrant,* means literally *"kick back"* (of a horse), and so contains precisely the same idea as the modern slang phrase *"a kicker".* Similarly *insult* goes back to a Lat. word meaning literally *"to jump on".* In earlier English slang is quite common. It is difficult to collect examples from O.E. because so little popular literature has come down from that age. But in M.E. there is no lack of picturesque, racy slang, often with a very modern ring. Chaucer's work is full of it. Thus in *Troilus and Criseyde* one of his characters, expostulating with another, says: *Al esily, for the love of Mars,* just as we might hear someone say today: *Take it easy, for the love of Mike* (or *Pete*). Of the Monk in the *Canterbury Tales* Chaucer writes:

> He *yaf nat* of that text *a pulled hen*
> That seith that hunters beth nat hooly men,

i.e. *he didn't give a plucked hen for the text,* just as we should say *"He didn't give a hoot",* etc. In the description of the Summoner we read: *And prively a fynch eek koude he pulle.* This expression, *"to pull* (pluck) *a finch"* is usually taken as the equivalent of Mod. *"rob a sucker",* though it may have a different and more sinister significance. Of the Pardoner Chaucer writes:

> He *made* the person (parson) and the peple *his apes,*

i.e. *he "made monkeys"* of them. He makes the duck, in *The Parlement of Foules* exclaim, rather inappropriately, *By my hat!* Many of the processes by which modern slang is created can be seen in Chaucer's writings. In the Elizabethan age slang is equally common, especially in the comic scenes in the plays. Any of Shakespeare's comedies and some of his historical plays will provide abundant material, for instance the speeches of Falstaff. The abusive tirade between Prince Hal and Falstaff in King Henry IV, Part 1, Act 2, Scene 4 contains a rich treasury of Elizabethan slang phrases. Some of the more picturesque are *clay-brained guts, knotty-pated fool, greasy tallow-catch* (*lump of tallow fat*), *bed-presser,* applied by the prince to his corpulent boon companion, and *starveling, eelskin, stockfish* used by Falstaff as a rejoinder. Ben Jonson's lively comedies of London life are full of racy slang; a few examples are *buzzard*, 'simple fellow', *catchpoll*, 'bailiff', *city-wires*, 'fashionable women', *coffin*, 'raised pie-crust', *hay in his horn*, 'bad-tempered', *suck*, 'cheat' (cf. Amer. *sucker*). In the eighteenth-century plays of Goldsmith and Sheridan there is plenty of slang, though in this age of correctness it perhaps lacks the exuberance of the Elizabethans. There is no need to point out specific examples of slang in the nineteenth and twentieth centuries; in certain modern writers it has become almost a cult; they seem to lean over backwards to avoid orthodox language.

The chief processes by which slang is produced can be seen in operation today as well as in the past. A large number of slang words are coined by modifying the form of more normal words; here the desire for novelty or for economy of utterance is at work. Thus frequently a word is shortened, either by cutting off the beginning or the end. This reduction has already been mentioned in *Prof.*, *Doc.*, to which may be added *pram*, *taxi(meter)*, *lab*, *gym*, *deb*, *pep(per)*, *fan(atic)*, *quint(uplet)s* or *quins*, etc. Earlier examples are *cab(riolet)*, *cad(et)*, *navvy*, (navigator—used in the sense of a labourer employed in excavation work). The first part of the word is dropped in *(tele)phone*, *(omni)bus*, *(peri)wig* (from Fr. *perruque*), *(di)sport*, etc. More radical dismemberment is seen in *p(e)ram(bulator)*, *(in)flu(enza)*, *bike* (*bicycle*), and *fridge* (Brit. for *refrigerator*), where sounds both in the middle and at the end have been lost. W. M. Rosetti in his *Reminiscences* tells us that his mother always said *cabriolet* and that *omnibus* was not "stripped" to *bus*. This was about 1830. Occasionally a phrase is reduced to initials. O.K., which has gained international currency, K.O., P.D.Q., N.G., S.A., B.O. (the latter perhaps technical rather than slang). Sometimes a sound is added, e.g. *kike*, probably from *Ike, Ike*; cf. earlier (e.g. Shakespearian) *nuncle* (*mine uncle*). Many of these words are no longer felt to be slang, e.g. *sport, wig, cab, bus*, which have become the accepted forms but were no doubt frowned on at one time. Now few people are aware that they have been shortened.

A process of shortening closely related to these is sometimes called "back-formation". It often produces another part of speech by the dropping of an ending. It has been used for both humorous and more serious coinages. Thus we have the colloquial verb *to burgle*, a back-formation from the noun *burglar*, *to jell* from *jelly*, *peeve(d)* from *peevish*, *to vamp* from *vampire*, and clichés such as *enthuse* from *enthusiasm*, and *opine* from *opinion*, etc. These are hardly considered good usage, but other words formed by the same method have been accepted, e.g. *beg* (an early back-formation from *beggar*), *pea* and *cherry* (formed from *peas(e)* and *cheris*—cf. Fr. *cérise*—owing to the mistaken idea that the *s* indicated a plural), *edit* from *editor*, *prizefight* from *prizefighter*. An interesting illustration of this process is seen in the verb *to grovel*, a back-formation from *grov(e)ling*, originally an adverb meaning *face downwards*. An attempt was made to coin a similar verb *darkle* from *darkling* (cf. Keats: *Darkling I listen*), but this did not succeed in establishing itself.

Oaths, which are a type of slang, are often distorted from their original form, partly to soften their effect, another case of euphemism. Thus we have the archaic *zounds* (*God's wounds*), *gadzooks* (*God's hooks*), *snails* (*God's nails*), referring no doubt to the hooks and nails used at the crucifixion. These picturesque expressions have died out; our modern swearing is less robust, but often reflects the same tendencies, e.g. *darned* or *dashed* as a more polite form of *damned*, *gee* for *Je(sus)*, *gosh* for

God, *crikey* for *Christ*, etc. An account of the changes of fashion in swearing during the ages would provide an interesting commentary both on the language and on social customs.

These rather mechanical distortions of words do not show the same degree of imagination reflected in other types of slang, though, as we see, they have been and still are productive of new words. A more interesting variety is the unconventional metaphor. Good modern examples are *highbrow* for *intellectual* and *lowbrow* for *non-intellectual*. These are perhaps not exact synonyms, as *highbrow* carries a slightly derogatory sense, but they are fairly close literary equivalents. *Highbrow* in Amer. Eng. seems to be losing ground at the moment to the still more unconventional *egghead*, also somewhat pejorative. American English has been particularly enterprising in coining this species of slang, a point discussed in more detail in Chapter 14. Certain objects and conditions seem to have lent themselves especially to this process of slang-creation at all times. Thus we have the numerous words, both early and modern, for the state of intoxication, a small fraction of which are mentioned above; the reader will have no difficulty in adding more. There is the large collection of expressions to denote mental deficiency; in addition to those already given one finds picturesque metaphors such as "*a screw (tile) loose*", "*bats in the belfry*", etc. Parts of the body, particularly the head, have many slang equivalents, as do topics such as money, unpopular people (of both sexes), in fact anything that has a strong human interest and can be treated in a humorous way.[3] Formerly the Model T Ford gave rise to many slang phrases, often of a somewhat ribald nature.[4]

[3] Interesting collections will be found in G. H. McKnight, *English Words and Their Background*, Chap. 4, and works on slang by Eric Partridge.

[4] See *American Speech*, Oct., 1931.

Another closely related process is the introduction of technical terms which are gradually used in a wider sense, and so become accepted as part of normal speech. This might also be considered as an example of the semantic change described as Widening of Meaning. The technical vocabulary of games and sports has provided a large number of terms, slang or at least colloquial, but often accepted now without the speaker being aware of their origin. Pugilism has given us *"a knock-out (blow)"*, *"take the count"*, *"down and out"*, *"punch-drunk"*, *"slap-happy"*, *"pulling his punches"*,[5] etc.; from poker we get *"to pass the buck"*, from skating *"to be on thin ice"*, from baseball *"to pinch-hit"* (act as substitute), from football (N. Amer.) *"to go into a huddle"* (have a consultation), from hunting *"to be in at the death"*, *"to be at fault"* (of a dog losing the scent), from racing *"a dark horse"*, *"to tip off"* (give a hint). The so-called sport of cock-fighting has left traces in *"to show the white feather"*, *"to have one's hackles up"* (appear aggressive), *"cock of the walk"*, etc. Other technical terms used in various professions and industries have sometimes obtained a wider currency. The army has given us *brass hat, barrage, camouflage, get the wind up, zero-hour, strafe,* all of which can be used nowadays in contexts that are not necessarily military. From flying we get *off the beam* and presumably from record-playing *in the groove.* From the movie we get *a close-up* and *a fade-out,* also in earlier days *a vamp.* The theatre gives us *in the limelight (spotlight),* a *"ham"* actor, a *"wow"* (great success), a *"flop"* (equally great failure). Mining has provided us with well-established phrases such as *"to peter out"*, *"to pan out"*. It will be noted that some of these expressions are colloquialisms rather than slang; they have been hallowed by time. *To pass the buck* and *to pinch-*

---

[5] Thus in 1939 an American senator said that the Allies were "pulling their punches".

hit are still modern and slangy; *to have one's hackles up* is sanctioned by age as a more respectable idiom.

Such freakish manipulations of words as "riming slang", e.g. "trouble and *strife*" for *wife*, or "reversed slang", e.g. *slop* for *police*, are not sufficiently wide-spread to leave any trace on the development of the language. Nor need "catch-words" be taken seriously, as they disappear after a short and often irritating life. The phrase "So's your old man", current some years ago, is now merely a linguistic fossil, and "cool cats", "squares" and "eggheads" may well meet the same fate.

These are a few of the processes which, both in the present and in the past, have given rise to slang and colloquialisms. They have added colour and variety to the language and do not altogether merit the righteous anger so often poured on them by the purist. There are, of course, arguments for and against the use of this informal speech. It brings vitality and freshness to the language. It often enables us to express briefly and pithily an idea that would need many more elaborate words in orthodox speech. We have only to attempt to translate a few current slang expressions into literary English to realize this. In the phrase *He was "all in"* the two expressive monosyllables would have to be replaced by "completely exhausted"; for the very useful modern term *debunk* we should have to say "strip off the false glamour" or "remove the illusions". *"To get by"* is to succeed with the minimum of effort. What can we substitute for *blurb*? This is surely a word that the language needed and will accept. The fact that distinguished writers do not scorn the occasional use of a slang phrase is also evidence of its appeal. Shaw sometimes has a slang expression—often an Americanism —in his virile prose. Galsworthy talks about *sob-stuff*, *swelled head*, *cold feet*. In these days of democratic mass-appeal through radio and television, eminent statesmen are not above this means of trying to reach the great heart of the people,[6] though, as we shall see in a later chapter, British orators often make howlers when trying to speak what they think is the American language. In the last general election in Britain the Conservative party made effective use of the slogan "You never had it so good", and on both sides of the Atlantic one hears and sees the phrase "go it alone" to indicate at a popular level what is more learnedly called "unilateral action".

Such are some of the merits of slang. Against them must be placed serious disadvantages. First, the very effectiveness and picturesqueness that have been praised are a danger; they provide too often a linguistic short cut, an automatic verbal response to a given situation that short-circuits thought. One admits readily that behind a great deal of our everyday conversation there is little active cerebration; the old definition of a sentence as "a complete thought" is far from accurate. Many of our ordinary remarks, the small change of social intercourse, are purely automatic, reflex actions in response to external stimuli. *How d'you do?*, *Hallo!*, *Fine day!*, *Awful weather!*, *Good morning* are little more than a verbal sign-language. But the danger of the continual use of slang is that it may become a substitute in cases where thought is really desirable. It may thus definitely discourage mental activity. Because of this it has been described as "the lazy man's dialect", "canned wisdom", or, more severely, "blank cheques of intellectual bankruptcy". Few things are so irritating as the person who has one or two adjectives, to whom everything is *swell* or *grand* or *fine* or *cute*, or else *terrible* or *awful* or *lousy*. Another drawback to slang is its ephemeral character; nothing is so dead as last year's slang phrase; the continual striving to be novel results in a high

[6] For examples see p. 194. Cf. Mr. Chamberlain's statement (1940): "Hitler has *missed the bus*".

rate of mortality in this department of speech, and so one has to be continually on the alert to be up-to-date. We ought then to be moderate in our use of slang and colloquialisms. As the language itself ultimately does, we should adopt those new creations which seem to fill a real need and reject those which merely have the meretricious attraction of novelty to recommend them. This implies an ability to make judgments and sometimes even prophecies, a gift not possessed by all, but at least we can develop a critical attitude towards these neologisms and not swallow them wholesale. Anyone who takes pride in his use of language must face this problem.

12. Other Processes of Word-Creation

We have now examined two important processes by which the vocabulary of a language is increased. First, there is the adoption of words from other languages, in the case of English perhaps the most usual method. Secondly, there is the development of informal language from various sources, as seen in the previous chapter. But this does not exhaust the possible ways of adding to the vocabulary, and some of the other modes by which new speech-material is created are described and illustrated here.

NEW COMPOUNDS

It is sometimes suggested that the O.E. habit of forming new expressions by combining two elements of the language was lost in later English. This is not true, although in Mod. E. this process is perhaps not used so freely as in O.E.; as has been noted, we depend more on foreign words for our new coinages, especially in the realm of science. But in all periods it has been possible to build up new words by joining two already-existing terms. Sometimes the new expression remains as two words, sometimes it is hyphenated, and sometimes the two words are fused into one. In this respect usage varies a good deal. Modern examples are . . . *pep-talk, call girl, takeover* (bid), *hangover, thruway, clearway* (Brit.), *hovercraft, Iron Curtain, Bamboo Curtain, gokart, loud-speaker, skyscraper, fanmail*, etc. Both elements in these compounds were well established in the vocabulary; by bringing them together a new word is made to denote a new idea. Similar formations are *moonlight*, *sunlight*, *starlight*, *airborne*, *air-tight*, *colour-blind*, *prizefight(er)*, *toothpick*, *fool-proof*, *waterproof* (noun and adj.), *air-minded* and the many compounds in *-minded*, and numerous other words. In poetry this has been a very fruitful source of new words, especially in the works of Shakespeare, Milton, Keats, Shelley, Tennyson.[1] Arresting and novel compounds are an important element in producing what is sometimes called "word-magic", e.g. Keats: "an *azure-lidded* sleep", "*purple-stained* mouth", "*spectre-thin*", Shelley: "*pestilence-stricken* multitudes", Tennyson: "*silken-sailed*", "*sullen-seeming* Death". Most of these poetical compounds are, however, coined for the occasion ("nonce-words") and have not become part of our normal vocabulary, even at the purely literary level.

Occasionally an apparent compound is not really what it seems; for instance *gridiron* has originally nothing to do with *iron*; its M.E. form was *gredire*, perhaps connected with *griddle*. The ending *-ire* was confused with *iron*, which also had a form *ire* in M.E., and so it was changed to *-iron*. This type of change by which a word or part of a word is given a more familiar form is well known in many languages and is called *folk-etymology* or *popular etymology*. Other examples in English are *crayfish* or *crawfish* from M.E. *crevice* (cf. Fr. *écrevisse*), the ending having been changed into Eng. *-fish*, *greyhound*, in which the first element has originally nothing to do with *grey*, *pick-axe* in which an ending *-ois*, *-oys* has been made into *-axe*, *penthouse*, M.E. *pentis*, a shortened form of *apentis*; cf. Lat. *appendix*. It is rather surprising to find that *penthouse* and *appendix* have a common origin. The name of

[1] See Bernard Groom, *The Formation and Use of Compound Epithets in English Poetry from* 1579, S.P.E. Tract XLIX.

the plant *tuberose* is not really a compound of *rose;* it is derived from a Lat. adjective *tuberosa,* meaning *swelling,* which should normally have given *tuberous,* with the same ending as *famous,* etc. A strange distortion is seen in *ale-wife,* the name of a North American fish, supposed to be derived from an Indian form *aloofe.*

Sometimes, on the other hand, compounds have taken on the appearance of a single word; we may call these disguised compounds. An example is the word *barn,* originally a combination of two words *bere,* 'barley' and *ærn,* 'a place', O.E. *bere-ern,* reduced in M.E. to *bern,* Mod. E. *barn.* Similarly the words *lord* and *lady* are very early compounds: *lord* < *hlāfweard,* 'loaf-keeper', already reduced to *hlāford* in O.E., *lady* composed of the same first element *hlāf* followed by an ending connected with a word meaning *to knead,* O.E. *hlǣfdīge,* the second part related to our word *dough. Lady* would therefore originally mean 'the loaf-kneader'. Other disguised compounds are *bridal,* O.E. *brȳd-ealo,* 'wedding-ale', *daisy,* O.E. *dæges ēage,* 'day's eye,' because this flower opens in the morning, *gospel* < *gōdspel,* 'good message', *gossip* < *godsibb,* 'relation in God', i.e. *godfather* or *godmother,* later degenerating in meaning, *handicap* 'hand in cap', formerly the name of a game, *hustings* from Scand. *hūsþing,* 'house-assembly', *sheriff,* O.E. *scīrgerēfa,* 'shire reeve', and many other terms. A "fused" compound of a verb+adverb is seen in the archaic forms *don* (< do on), *doff* (< do off). Earlier English also had *dout* (< do out), used in the sense of "put out, extinguish".

Addition of Prefixes or Suffixes

Sometimes, instead of combining two independent words, the new expression is built up by adding a prefix

or an ending to a word. Thus in adapting Ger. *übermensch*
G. B. Shaw added the prefix *super–*, as in *superlative*,
to *man*, and a new term *superman* was added to the language. In the same way, to denote a type of humanity
inferior to man as he now exists the opposite prefix *sub–*
is used, giving us *subman*. These two prefixes have been
attached to many other words: *superstructure, supertax,
supercharge, super-Dreadnought, supermarket*, etc. In
fact this process is so well recognized that one may hear
super itself used to indicate supreme excellence. To say
that a thing is *super* is somewhat the same as saying it is
de luxe, in the language of those who enjoy clichés. The
film has no doubt contributed to the spread of this prefix,
but when every film has become a super-film a new term
has to be invented. One might recommend *superexcellent*,
which it is surprising to find has been in the language
from 1561 and does not date from the Hollywood age.
Similarly *sub–* has given *subway, sub-zero, subnormal,
subpolar, subtropic(al), subconscious(ness), submarine,
sub-deb.*, etc. The prefix *co–* has been very productive,
e.g. *cooperation, coexistence, coeducation(al)*, with the
popular abbreviation *co-ed*, which quite illogically denotes
only the feminine student. These three prefixes are derived from Latin, but English prefixes may equally well
be used in this way. Thus *under–* gives us *undersea, un-
dersize, undernourish(ed), underarm, underbid, under-
wear, –clothes*, etc.; *over* gives *overbid, overcall, overarm,
overact, overall(s), overcapitalize, overcoloured, overdose*,
etc. These words might, of course, equally well be considered as compounds of independent words, as *under*
and *over*, unlike *super* and *sub*, exist as separate units, but
their function in such words as those given is rather that
of a prefix. These prefixes and many others may be called
"productive" because new words can still easily be made

with their help. Other prefixes have ceased to produce new compounds, e.g. *for–*, *be–*, or at least they do so very sparingly; *belittle* is a relatively late coinage, of U.S. origin, much criticized at one time as an Americanism but now accepted. The particles *pre–* and *pro–* are fairly productive, e.g. *pre-history*, *–historic*, *pre-digest* (which it is surprising to note goes back to 1663), *pre-war*, and *pro-tariff*, *pro-German*, *pro-cathedral* (a church used as a cathedral).

Suffixes may be used in the same way. Thus the ending *–ster* has been added to form new words such as *punster*, *oldster*, *youngster*, *trickster*, *gangster*, and *roadster*; often, though not always, it conveys a slightly derogatory meaning. The ending *–er* is still more common as a productive suffix: *booster*, *kicker*, *knocker*, *mixer*, *header*, *zipper*, *crooner*, etc. The suffixes *–ism*, *–ize*, (*ise*), *–ist*, and *–ite* yield many new words: *jingoism*, *nazism*, *fascism*, *socialism*, *communism*, *bolshevism*, *alcoholism*, *Darwinism*, *conservatism*, *liberalism* and innumerable other *–isms*. The person who adopts these *–isms* is often an *–ist*, sometimes an *–ite*; in England the ending *–ite* often conveys a somewhat slighting suggestion, e.g. *labourite* (which seems to be a neutral term in N. Amer.), though *Jacobite*, *Semite* carry no derogatory implication. The ending *–ize* or *–ise* has produced a large number of new words and is still a living suffix, especially in N. Amer. It is often attached to names of peoples, e.g. *Anglicize*, *Americanize*, *Gallicize*, etc. More general uses are seen in *colonize*, *monopolize*, *philosophize*, *moralize*, *actualize*, *galvanize*, *oxidize*. N. Amer. has given us *hospitalize*, *institutionalize*, etc. The suffix *–age* can still be used in the production of new words, e.g. *coverage*, *sabotage*. Both these words emerged in the present century, the latter built up from the Fr. *sabot*, a shoe, because shoes were used to wreck machinery. *Roughage* and *wreckage* were coined in the nineteenth century; both are "hybrids", the Fr. ending *–age* having been attached to a Teutonic root, though *wreck* seems to have come into M.E. through Fr. The ending *–ish* has been combined with words to form adjectives; a development of this suffix in colloquial speech (mainly British) is its use to indicate about a certain time or a certain number of years, e.g. *Come about threeish, She's fortyish.* This is probably just a passing fashion; it already shows signs of dying out. The ending *–ee* is still productive; recent creations are *standee, evacuee, trainee.* Certain endings, especially the abstract-forming *–dom, –hood, –th,* are not very productive in Mod. E., though we may note *Tsardom* and Mr. Churchill's *Nazidom* (1940) by the side of the more usual *Nazism.* Another suffix with much the same function, *–ery,* has given a number of new words, especially in N. Amer., e.g. *thuggery, bootery, eatery* on the model of *grocery, slavery,* etc. Ruskin's attempt to introduce the term *illth* as the opposite of *wealth* did not succeed, and *coolth* on the analogy of *warmth* is only jocular. The suffix *–ship* has been popular as a result of a book called *Gamesmanship* and has given us *brinkmanship* as an element in the cold war. From *marathon* have been modelled such terms as *talkathon, walkathon,* etc., and the Russian affix *–nik* has given us *beatnik,* the first syllable.

These are only a very few prefixes and suffixes out of the large number in the language, and the examples of words created by them have been taken mainly from Mod. E. It is obvious that if we were to examine the whole of this group of particles and assess the contributions they are responsible for in the different periods of the language, we should include a great many words in our present vocabulary.

WORDS FORMED FROM NAMES OF PERSONS

Many new words derived from proper nouns have been added to the language at various times. Both persons and places have given their names to ideas and objects with which they have been associated. Thus today some people prefer to denote the so-called Oxford group, which has no real connection with Oxford, by the term *Buchmanites*, after its leader, and its tenets *Buchmanism*. During World War II, the Air Force needed a name for an inflatable vest-like life-preserver and some linguistic genius christened it a *Mae West*. Two Scotsmen, Macadam and Mackintosh, have their names enshrined in the type of road and waterproof garment that they invented, and an architect named Hansom gave his name to the vehicle that flourished in the Victorian age and was called by Disraeli "the gondola of London". First it was called a "hansom" cab, later simply a *hansom*. In the eighteenth century a *sandwich* was named after the Earl of Sandwich, who once spent twenty-four hours at the gambling table on a steady diet of beef sandwiches; *grog*, shortened from *grogram*, was the nickname of the admiral who discovered this drink and introduced it into the navy, who had previously taken their rum cold. The same century also sees the introduction of *lynch law*, said to be named after a Captain Lynch of Virginia. In the nineteenth century we have *boycott*, so called because Captain Boycott was the first victim of this technique, and *to burke* (to stifle a discussion), a grim reminder of a notorious murderer, who, with his accomplice Hare, carried out a series of crimes in Edinburgh. The quotation from the London *Times* given in the *Shorter Oxford Dictionary* describing how the crowd present at the public execution shouted: "*Burke him, Burke him!*" indicates vividly how this meaning arose. The U.S. term *gerrymander*, referring to an unfair method of arranging elections, has as its first element the name of a Governor of Massachusetts, Elbridge Gerry. The words *sadism, sadist(ic)* are coined from the name of the notorious Marquis (really Count) de Sade; *masochism* is from Sacher-Masoch, an Austrian novelist.

Older examples of the same process are seen in *tawdry, dunce* and *maudlin*. *Tawdry* is from *(Sain)t Audrey* or *Ethelrida,* originally referring to a lace neck-cloth associated with this Saint, and then, because this feminine adornment was often cheap and showy, developing its present meaning in the seventeenth century. The word *dunce* is from John *Duns* Scotus, a learned theologian who died in 1308. After his teachings went out of fashion the term Dunses, applied to his followers, took on a derogatory meaning, which survives in our modern word *dunce*. *Maudlin* is from (Mary) Magdalen, who is often portrayed as weeping. It will be noted that all these words have degenerated in meaning.

A number of scientific terms have been coined from personal names, especially in botany; their varied origin throws an interesting sidelight on the international character of science. Thus we find *dahlia* (from Dahl, a Swedish botanist), *fuchsia* (Fuchs, a German), *forsythia* (Forsyth, an Englishman), *wistaria* (Wistar or Wister, an American). In physics we have *watt* (James Watt, a Scotsman), *ohm* (E. S. Ohm, a German), *volt* (Volta, an Italian), *ampère* (Ampère, a Frenchman).[2] The names of a benefactor to humanity and a pseudo-scientist are crystallized in *pasteurize* (Louis Pasteur) and *mesmerize* (Mesmer, an Austrian charlatan).

Sometimes names of literary characters have provided us with new words. Familiar examples are *quixotic*, from

[2] See Greenough and Kittredge, *Words and Their Ways in English Speech*, p. 384.

Don Quixote, *to pander*, from Pandarus, the go-between in the legend of Troilus and Cressida (Chaucer's form is *Pandare*), *gamp* (colloquial for umbrella) from 'Sairy' Gamp in *Martin Chuzzlewit*, the tough nurse who carried a cotton umbrella, a *jobation* or *jawbation*, meaning a long, tedious lecture such as Job had to listen to from his friends. We can also call a person a Shylock, a Romeo, a gay Lothario, a Micawber, a Jezebel, a Job's comforter, etc. Names in classical history and legend have also contributed new items to the vocabulary. Thus an *epicure* derives his name from Epikouros, the Greek whose philosophy was associated with the idea of the pursuit of pleasure; *platonic* is connected with the doctrines of Plato; *Socratic, cynic, stoic* also reflect ancient creeds and schools of philosophy. The word *draconic* (severe, strict) is formed from Draco, an Athenian to whom is attributed a severe code of laws.

WORDS FORMED FROM NAMES OF PLACES

Place-names have also given rise to new words. The Mod. slang word *bunk* (*debunk*) is a shortened form of Bunkum or Buncombe, the name of a county in N. Carolina, whose member insisted on making a speech, no matter how futile, because Buncombe expected it. A *pistol* is derived from the name Pistoia, a town in Tuscany, a *bayonet* is possibly from Bayonne in France. Many names of wines are connected with the places where they are produced or exported: *port* (Oporto), *sherry*, earlier *sherris* (Xeres), *champagne*, *tokay* (a town in Hungary), *hock* (Hochheim, Germany), etc. Certain articles of food obtain their names in the same way: *turkey, currant*, from Corinth, *sardine* possibly from Sardinia, *tangerine* (orange) from Tangiers, *cantaloup* from Ital. Cantalupe, a former country home of the Pope near Rome, where this species of melon was cultivated. Various cloths and other materials take their names from the places associated with them: *arras* and *cretonne* from French towns with those names, *damask* from Damascus, *muslin* from a town in Mesopotamia, *cashmere* and *calico* from India, *worsted* from Worstead in Norfolk, England, *cambric* from Cambray in Flanders, etc. The *canary* is named from the Canary Islands.

Classical place-names as well as personal names have been embedded in our vocabulary. Thus a *sybarite* (a luxurious, effeminate person) takes his name from Sybaris, an ancient Greek city notorious for its luxury and effeminacy, *laconic* is derived from Laconia, whose chief city Sparta has also given us *spartan;* the ideas behind the two words are not unlike, except that *laconic* is applied to brief and disciplined speech. Other examples of words derived from names of persons and places can easily be found. Their discovery and explanation is one of the most fascinating problems in the history of language and reveals associations that are often quite unsuspected.

SPONTANEOUS MODES OF WORD-CREATION

Finally there is a group of words in the vocabulary that seems to have arisen spontaneously; often no specific source can be assigned to them. An interesting collection can be made of the numerous echoic or onomatopoeic terms, words which are supposed to reproduce natural sounds. An interesting modern example, chiefly N. Amer., is *wow*, apparently an attempt to reproduce in a word the noise made by an excited and appreciative audience. Later it is attached to the performance that evokes this exclamation of approval, and we can say in the colloquial language: It's a *wow* (a great success). *Zip* and *zipper* are also modern instances of the same process; *zip* echoes a sound, and the term *zipper* is then built up from this. Other words of this type are *bang, boom, hiss, splash* (earlier *plash*), *squeak, squeal, wheeze, whizz, hiccup* (earlier *hickock*)—sometimes wrongly spelt *hiccough* by "popular etymology". These are all obviously attempts to indicate certain noises. The words used as the calls of animals are in the same category: *mew, miaow, mewl, quack, neigh, moo, grunt, hee-haw*, etc.: *bow-wow* and *cock-a-doodle-doo* are rather remote from the actual sounds. The *cuckoo* gets its name in the same way, as do the *chickadee*, the *whippoorwill* and many other birds.

Other words have been coined by individual writers. Lewis Carroll (C. L. Dodgson) showed great powers of invention in his *Alice* books, but few of his new words have gained wide currency. The best known is probably *chortle*, which is an interesting example of what is sometimes called a portmanteau word or, more simply, a "blend". By this is meant the fusion of two words into one by using a part of each. Thus *chortle* is supposed to be a blend of *chuckle* and *snort*, the beginning of the first word being combined with the latter part of the second. Another example is *brunch*, a combination of *breakfast* and *lunch*, i.e. a late breakfast or an early lunch taken as the first meal of the day. *Amerindian* for *American Indian*, *cinemaddict* for *cinema addict*, *electrocute* (electric+execute), *travelogue* (travel+monologue), *smog* (smoke+fog), *motel* (motor+hotel) are examples of more recent "blends". Formations like *socialite, motorcade, newscast*, etc., may be considered as blends or as illustrations of the extension of suffixes, a process already discussed. *Motorcade* is based on *cavalcade, newscast* on *broadcast*. A purely American coinage is *happenstance* (happening+circumstance); *paratroopers* and *breathalyser* other recent examples in this category. The new word *blurb* is the useful coinage of an American writer; it too is probably a blend.

The more recent work of James Joyce contains many words of his own invention, often showing a good deal of ingenuity, but it is doubtful whether many of them will survive. Examples from *Finnegan's Wake* are: *foamous* old Dobbelin ayle; the *shoutmost shoviality*; a *bleaueye-deal*, an *anamorous* letter. Their meaning is sometimes not so easy to guess as the Carrollian neologisms.

THE DICTIONARY AT THE BREAKFAST TABLE

In this chapter and some of the earlier ones we have explored the most important methods by which our vocabulary has gradually been built up. Let us take a group of common words and notice how varied is their origin; it will provide us with a microcosm of the language. We are at the breakfast table. The name of the meal itself is an example of a compound formed by combining two native Eng. words, but if it were *dinner* or *supper* we should be using words of Fr. origin. We begin with a *grape-fruit*, another compound, this time two words of Fr. origin but put together on American soil. Or it may be *an orange*, in which case we have an Arabic word *naranj*, which should have given us *a norange* (not infrequently heard); by a well-known process—cf. *an adder*, which should be *a nadder*—the *n* has been subtracted from the word and added to the article *a*. In summer we may have a *melon* (Fr. from Greek) or a *cantaloup*, named, as we have seen, after an Italian town. This is followed by a *cereal*, in which is enshrined the name of *Ceres*, the Roman goddess of agriculture. It may be the old-fashioned *porridge*, a secondary form of *pottage* (Fr.) or a synthetic substance with an equally synthetic modern composite trade-name such as *crispies*, illustrating the extension of the *-ie* suffix (cf. *goodies*, *nighties*, etc.). Next, if it is a solid English breakfast, comes *bacon*, an example of the names of meats taken over from Fr., and *eggs*, a Scandinavian loan-word. This is accompanied by *bread*, an O.E. word with a Scand. meaning attached to it, and *butter* (Eng. from Lat.) or *toast* (Fr.) and *marmalade*, a Portuguese word probably imported through Fr., or *jam*, apparently an onomatopoeic or echoic word. We drink *tea*, a Chinese word perhaps introduced from Malayan Dutch, *coffee* (Arabic), which may be *mocha*, the name of an Arabian port, or perhaps we take *cocoa*, a Spanish-Mexican word. We sit at a *table* (Fr.) on a *chair* (Fr.) and have in front of us a *knife* (Eng.), *fork* (Eng. from Lat.) and *spoon* (Eng.), *plates* (Fr.), a *cup* (Eng. from Lat.) and *saucer* (Fr.). There is a *table-cloth* (a compound of Fr. and Eng.) and a *napkin* (a hybrid with a Fr. root and an Eng. ending) or if we prefer to employ a euphemism and be genteel, a *serviette* (Fr.). After our *meal* (Eng.) we light a *cigarette* (Span.) with a *match* (Fr.), catch a *bus* (Lat. abbreviation), a *street-car* (Eng.—from Lat.—and Fr.), or a *tram* (Low Ger.) and go to our day's work.

So in this small group of everyday words we range from Roman mythology to Arabic, from the Romance languages French, Spanish and Portuguese to the Teutonic, Scandinavian and Low German tongues, with a substratum of native English or Anglo-Saxon. Persons and places contribute their quota to the terminology, and the different modes of forming composites are represented. In other departments of the vocabulary the same variety of sources can easily be seen. It is no exaggeration to talk about the romance of words.

13. British and American English; Pronunciation, Forms and Syntax

Though the study of American English has received a great deal of attention in recent years, the differences between it and British English have long been recognized, both by the populace and by scholars. There is a story, possibly apocryphal, of a Parisian shop that displayed a sign: *English spoken; American understood*. Some years ago, at an exhibition in London, a list of terms was drawn up for the benefit of visiting Americans who had run into difficulties because of the peculiarities of British speech: Eng. *braces*, Amer. *suspenders*; *petrol*, *gas(oline)*; *nib*, *penpoint*; *(boot)lace*, *shoe-string*; *sweets*, *candy*; *drawing-pins*, *thumbtacks*, and so on. At certain American plays in England the programme provides an explanation of the more difficult words and phrases, especially slang and colloquialisms. Some of Sinclair Lewis's books have been produced in England with a glossary of Americanisms.

In the academic world there is also evidence of a growing interest in this subject. In 1919 Mr. Mencken wrote a lively book with the provocative title, *The American Language*, a work that has gone through several editions and been widely read. The late Professor Krapp of Columbia University published a large monograph in two volumes with the more cautious title *The English Language in America*. The University of Chicago has produced its large-scale *Dictionary of American English*, which contains a wealth of lexical information about the English language on the North American continent. It was edited

by Sir William Craigie, a former editor of the Oxford
English Dictionary. When the news of Sir William's
appointment was announced, a Chicago newspaper, wish-
ing to use the language he was going to investigate, had as
a headline *Midway Signs Limey Prof to Dope Yank
Talk.* For several years a periodical, *American Speech*, has
appeared dealing with various aspects of American English, especially its latest developments and new coinages.
A companion volume to the useful *Modern English Usage*
has been written under the title *Modern American Usage.*
Two detailed studies of American pronunciation have
been made, one by Krapp, the other by H. S. Kenyon. A
large-scale investigation of North American speech, *The
Linguistic Atlas of the United States and Canada,* is well
under way, and several volumes of maps have already been
published. A number of comprehensive works on American slang have been compiled.

This attempt to establish and obtain recognition of a
special form of speech for America is not confined to
modern times. Ever since the war of independence voices
have arisen in protest against the linguistic connection
with Great Britain. The tone of these attacks in earlier
times was often violent. It is said that one fervid patriot
at first suggested that America should entirely abandon
the English language and adopt Hebrew as her national
tongue. Then Greek was mentioned as the new language,
but the opponents of this idea said England might take
Greek as her language and America retain English. Even
Noah Webster, though he did not go so far as to advocate
the substitution of another language for English, showed
in his *Dissertations on the English Language,* published
in 1789, the same chauvinistic attitude. He prophesied
that, owing to the separation of the two countries, there
would arise in the course of time "a language in North
America as different from the future language of England

as the modern Dutch, Danish or Swedish are from the German, or from one another." So far Webster's prophecy, like so many others about linguistic matters, has not proved correct; he could not foresee the great advance in means of communication and other factors that would hinder this process of differentiation. In the same work Webster says: "As a nation we have a very great interest in *opposing* the introduction of any plan of uniformity with the British language." And from the end of the eighteenth century down to the present day there have been many American writers who have adopted this extreme view. Whitman's views in his *American Primer* are characteristic: "Ten thousand native idiomatic words are growing, or are already grown, out of which vast numbers could be used by American writers, with meaning and effect—words which would give that taste of identity and locality which is so dear in literature, words that would be welcomed by the nation, being of the national blood." This is clearly a type of linguistic nationalism.

At the same time in England equally serious criticisms were being made of Americanisms. One could collect amusing examples of bitter condemnation of American expressions such as *belittle, lengthy*, which are now accepted on both sides of the Atlantic without a murmur. The tone of these discussions is gradually improving; the fiery note of the earlier controversies has happily almost disappeared, though occasionally there is an immoderate outburst from one side or the other, generally in the writings of unqualified persons who set themselves up as judges.

There is of course no reason why the nature of British and American English should not be examined coolly and objectively like any other linguistic problem. We merely have to put aside our personal prejudices, which is perhaps not so easy as it sounds, and examine the two types of English just as a scientist investigates two different species of animals or plants. He does not allow his emotions to affect his enquiry, and the student of language has to adopt the same course. In making this comparison we have to answer questions such as the following: (1) What exactly is meant by British and American English? (2) What are the main differences between these two varieties of English? (3) What is the origin of these differences? (4) Are they increasing or decreasing? (5) Is the variation sufficiently great to justify the term "the American language"? A detailed discussion of these points would fill a large book; only a brief survey can be given here.

THE TERMS BRITISH AND AMERICAN ENGLISH

To define British and American English is not an easy task; it might even be argued that there are no such entities. In reality there exist, both in Great Britain and in North America, a large number of different dialects, theoretically as many dialects as there are individuals, because actually no two people use a form of speech that is quite identical. We may even go further and say that the same person does not always speak the same dialect; his language will vary considerably according to circumstances; in addressing a large gathering he will not use the same type of language as in informal conversation with one or two intimate friends. A native of a country village changes his speech, often quite unconsciously, when talking to a stranger from the city. But obviously we cannot examine all these varieties of a language, and usually one type is singled out for description and comparison. In the case of British English the so-called Standard language is generally taken. This is of course not an entirely uniform dialect, but it is fairly definite, and is wide-spread among people of a certain social background and education irrespective of the region they come from. Its origin has already been indicated.[1] It is sometimes called "Public School English", the term "Public School" being used in the British sense of private school. It is probably what is referred to as the "Oxford accent", though this term is at once too wide and too narrow. There are dons and undergraduates at Oxford who do not speak Standard English and there are many people who have had no connection with Oxford who use this form of speech. But, although there is some vagueness about the term and though even within Standard English there is considerable fluctuation, it is a fairly definite dialect and has been described in detail in several books.[2] It is perhaps best defined negatively, as that form of British speech which does not reveal the speaker's geographical origin. It must be emphasized that no attempt is made here to suggest that Standard English is inherently superior to other forms of English, either in Great Britain or abroad.[3] It is simply one dialect of English, which, it must be admitted, carries with it a certain amount of social prestige. On the other hand, many speakers who do not possess this dialect have risen to the highest offices of State and Church. No true Scotsman would admit that his Scottish dialect was inferior to Standard English. The question of values must be set aside.

To select one of the numerous American dialects for comparison is not an easy task. Although the range of dialectal variation is probably smaller, there is nothing in

[1] See p. 74.
[2] E.g. D. Jones, *Outline of English Phonetics*, I. C. Ward, *The Phonetics of English*, A. Lloyd James, *Our Spoken Language*, etc.
[3] The thesis of the superiority of St. Eng. as a means of expression has been maintained by H. C. Wyld, *The Best English*, S.P.E. Tract No. 39.

North America quite parallel to the Standard speech of Great Britain. There are obvious reasons for this: first, the absence of the "Public School" system on this continent; secondly, the vaguer social boundaries and the easier circulation between classes, factors which prevent the development of a class dialect such as Standard English. But several writers on American pronunciation have analyzed what is called General American or Central American speech or even Standard English in America.[4] This is the type of American speech which, as its name suggests, is spread over a large portion of the North American continent. It might also be called Northern American, which is spoken in the most thickly populated portion of the U.S.A. (except in New England) and is influencing Western and Southern speech. In contrast to it are the Eastern and Southern American dialects. These are the peripheral forms of speech heard in New England and the Southern States; outside these regions there is a fairly uniform type of speech extending over the central and western portion of the U.S.A. and Canada, which we may conveniently call General American, the closest approach to the Standard English of Great Britain. In comparing British and American English we are therefore comparing these two dialects of Great Britain and North America. To compare all the various dialects of the two regions would be an enormous task, for which the materials are not available; we have too little information at present about dialects on both sides of the Atlantic, though the work of the *Linguistic Atlas of the U.S. and Canada* is filling up gaps in our knowledge of North American speech.

[4] See J. S. Kenyon, *American Pronunciation*, G. P. Krapp, *The Pronunciation of Standard English in America*, T. Larsen and F. S. Walker, *Pronunciation; a Practical Guide to Spoken English in Canada and the United States*, Hans Kurath, *American Pronunciation*, S.P.E. Tract No. 30.

DIFFERENCES BETWEEN BRITISH (STANDARD ENG.) AND "GENERAL" AMERICAN SPEECH

In examining these differences it will be convenient to classify them as variations in pronunciation, forms, syntax and vocabulary. Forms and syntax show little variation, pronunciation and vocabulary considerably more. It is generally these that betray the origin of a speaker.

At the outset a clear distinction must be drawn between the two or three levels of language that were described in Chapter 11, literary, colloquial and slang. It will be found that, as we pass from the lower to the higher level, the variations between British and American English decrease. It is in popular speech, and in that speech as recorded in literature, that Americanisms and Briticisms are frequent. If we examine the work of earlier writers such as Emerson, Irving, Hawthorne, even Whitman, who, as we have seen, prided himself on his use of American locutions, or modern writers such as Hergesheimer, Willa Cather, Sinclair Lewis, Dreiser, Hemingway, Steinbeck, we find, in the descriptive, narrative and argumentative portions of their books, very little that is definitely American, except of course in references to specifically American natural objects or institutions, e.g. *chipmunk, chautauqua*. As soon, however, as they reproduce popular speech in their dialogue the style changes immediately and an unmistakable American colouring is present. Certain American writers, e.g. Ring Lardner, Damon Runyon, following a long tradition in American literature, have attempted to use this popular speech—or what they imagine is popular speech—as a literary medium, but it is doubtful whether this will have any permanent effect on the language of American literature. Some of the ultra-colloquial dialogue in O. Henry's stories is already unin-

telligible to the younger generation. The situation can be
indicated by the accompanying diagram.

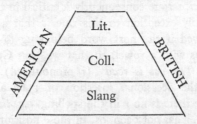

It is interesting to notice that Mencken, the most eloquent advocate of the doctrine of American linguistic independence, shows little that is exclusively American in
his effective and vigorous writings. His style is as forthright
as Bernard Shaw's—indeed there is considerable similarity
between these two literary *enfants terribles*—but it is
scarcely more American. A perusal of the first twenty-five
pages of the third edition of *The American Language* does
not reveal a single word or idiom that could not be equally
well used by a contemporary English writer except possibly *maybe* for *perhaps*, a *peek* for a *peep*, though even
these are not labelled U.S. by the Oxford Dictionary. But
as we descend from this level to colloquialism and slang,
as far as these can be separated from literary expressions,
the divergence will tend to increase. It is only at these
lower levels that there could be any serious difficulty of
communication between Britishers and Americans.

DIFFERENCES IN PRONUNCIATION
Consonants

If the pronunciation of Standard English (St. Eng.) is
compared with General American (Am. E.) certain con-
trasts emerge. In the consonants the chief difference is in
the treatment of the *r*-sound. In St. Eng. this has been

completely lost finally and before other consonants, e.g. in words such as *car*, *fir*, or *card*, *first*. The two words *father* and *farther* are consequently identical in pronunciation. The only exception to this rule is that a final *r* is often preserved if the next word belonging to the same phrase begins with a vowel, so that we hear *Get the car* (no *r*) but *The car is ready* (*r* pronounced). This accounts for the occasional insertion of *r* by analogy in Br. E. where there is no *r* in the spelling, e.g. *the idear of it*. In Am. E. *r* has not been lost in these positions, though it is not so definite a consonant as in the beginning of a word; in fact it sometimes survives only as a vague colouring of the preceding vowel. In Gen. Amer. *father* and *farther* are not homonyms. It should be noted, however, that many Eastern and Southern American speakers treat the *r* in much the same way as in St. Eng.

Another difference in the consonants is the absence, in many, though not all, speakers of St. Eng., of any distinction between initial *w* and *wh*. Thus words such as *which* and *witch* are identical, as are *when* and *wen*, *where* and *were*, *whether* and *weather*; *why* is pronounced like the name of the letter *y*. In Am. E. *wh*– generally has a different sound from *w*–.

A wide-spread consonantal variation is heard in words such as *new(s)*, *Tuesday*, *student*, where Br. E. has a *y* sound before the vowel. In Am. E. this sound is often absent, giving a pronunciation *noo(s)*, *stoodent*, etc. This, however, is by no means universal. On the other hand the *y*-less pronunciation is general in Br. E. in *figure*, *column*; a *y* may sometimes be heard in these words in Am. E., especially in the southern dialects.

There are other minor variations in the consonants in these two forms of speech, but these affect relatively few words, e.g. *schedule* (Br. E. *sh*–, Am. E. *sk*–, though *sh*– is occasionally heard in Am. E.); *herb*, where Am. E. frequently has a silent *h*, while Br. E. has restored the *h*; *vase*, *raspberry*, where the *s* is pronounced *z* in Br. E., occasionally *s* in Am. E.; *lieutenant*, Br. E. *left–*, Am. E. *loot–*.

Vowels

The most striking difference between the vowels of St. Eng. and Am. E. speech is that heard in such words as *pass, laugh, bath, plant, half,* etc. where St. Eng. has the so-called "broad *a*", which is not generally present in Am. E. Various sounds are used instead, most speakers having a vowel that is identical with the sound in *cat, man*; others, especially in eastern New England,[5] use a vowel intermediate between this and the St. Eng. sound. This, it might be noted in passing, is one of the traps into which the speaker who sets out to acquire a St. Eng. accent nearly always falls. He learns to say *class* with a "broad" *a* and then unfortunately carries it over into *classics* and *classical*, where it does not belong; in these two words St. Eng. has the same *a* as in *cat*. He learns to say *drahma* and then says *drahmatist*, which in St. Eng. has the same vowel as *dram*. He cultivates a broad *a* in *pass* but does not realize that St. Eng. has a different vowel in *passage* and *trespass* or that the vowel in *mass* and *Catholic* is not the same as in *pass* and *bath*. An over-enthusiastic adherent of the broad *a* may even be heard to say: *Turn on the gahs!* It is not easy to modify one's dialect; to do so perfectly is almost as difficult as to learn a foreign language.

Another wide-spread vowel difference can be detected in the "short *o*" sound as in *not, block, rod*. Here Am. E. often, though not always, has an "unrounded" vowel, approximately the same as the *a* of *father*, but shorter. St.

---

[5] See Chart, p. 213.

Eng. has a vowel with slight lip-rounding, fairly close to the sound in *saw, nor.* Some American speakers, however, use a rounded and lengthened vowel in certain words where St. Eng. has this short *o*, e.g. *dog, swan.* There is considerable variation in this group of words, even among speakers of Gen. Amer.; in St. Eng. the pronunciation is fairly uniform.

The "long *o*" sound is generally much more diphthongized in St. Eng. than in Am. E., e.g. *go, home.* In St. Eng. it begins with a modified *o* sound but ends with the sound of *u* in *put.* This diphthongization is increasing in England and seems to be developing in the speech of many Americans, though not to the same degree. The vowel in *day, name* is also diphthongized, though here the difference between Br. E. and Am. E. is not so marked.

The "short *u*" sound as in *but, come* has a different quality in St. Eng. and Am. E. This is especially noticeable before *r*, e.g. *hurry, courage,* where the sound is often considerably modified in Gen. Amer.

The pronunciation of a number of words with *er* (*ear*) differs in Br. E. and Am. E. In *clerk* St. Eng. has the sound *ar* (*ah*), Am. E. the sound *er.* This variation shows itself in a group of proper names, e.g. *Derby, Berkshire, Berkeley. Derby,* pronounced with *er,* is also used in Am. E. to denote a *hat* (=Eng. *bowler*). The word *hearth* occasionally has the *er* sound in Am. E., especially in older dialect speakers. According to Krapp, the only word in which *er* is pronounced *ar* in Am. E. is *sergeant.*[6]

Differences in the accentuation of words give rise to many variations between the two forms of speech. Sometimes the difference in the position of the accent causes a modification of the vowel sounds, e.g. Br. E. *enQUIry,* with stress on the second syllable and a "long *i*", by the side of Am. E. *INquiry,* often with stress on the first syl-

[6] G. P. Krapp, *The English Language in America,* vol. II, p. 37.

lable and "short *i*" in the second, Br. E. *adDRESS*, with stress on *–dress* and a slurred first syllable, and often stress on *ad–* and a "full vowel" in Am. E. The same change can be seen in a word like *primarily*, where Br. E. has the stress on *pri–* and the *a* of the second syllable is slurred, as compared with the frequent American pronunciation with the stress on *mar* and a "full vowel" in this syllable. *Temporarily* shows the same variation. In other words, there is little change in the vowels in spite of the frequent difference in stress, e.g. Br. E. *magazINE*, Am. E. *MAGazine*, Br. E. *specTATor*, Am. E. *SPECtator*, Br. E. *roMANCE*, Am. E. *ROmance*, Br. E. *reCESS*, Am. E. *REcess*. The general tendency here seems to be for the accent to be placed on the first syllable in Am. E. This process shows itself in Br. E. too, e.g. *adult*, *ally*, where the stress is moving to the first syllable, but it is not so common as in Am. E.

Even in words where the accent falls in the same place in Am. E. and Br. E. there is often a good deal of variation because of the greater tendency in St. Eng. to slur unstressed syllables. Take the word *extraordinary*. It is said that the speaker of St. Eng. pronounces it as one syllable. This is of course an exaggeration, but he may and often does reduce it to two syllables, *kstrordnri*, a difficult though not impossible feat. The more painstaking American speaker frequently has six syllables; this means that usually two secondary accents are introduced, one on *ex*, the other on *ar*, and that these syllables, instead of losing their vowels as in St. Eng., are pronounced with "full" vowels. This phenomenon, the presence of "full" vowels in Amer. speech where St. Eng. has slurred vowels or none at all, is very far-reaching and perhaps accounts for the most striking differences between the two dialects. It is this as much as anything that arouses mutual criticism; the Englishman is accused of "swallowing" his words, while the American pronunciation, though more distinct, sounds rather monotonous to the English ear because of the frequent occurrence of full vowels. It produces the effect of an absence of light and shade in speech, a too uniform stress. But these aesthetic and subjective judgments will obviously depend so largely on what the listener has been used to and his own speech-habits that they are of little value.

This process of reduction in unstressed syllables is particularly noticeable in the British pronunciation of names. Both consonants and vowels are affected. The *–ham* of English towns is reduced to *–em* with a "neutral" vowel. To pronounce *Birmingham* with a final syllable like the independent word *ham* or *Portsmouth* with the same sound as in *mouth* sounds very unnatural to the English ear, just as strange as the pronunciation of *Illinois* with a final *s* sounds to those American speakers who drop this final sound. Similarly *Greenwich* becomes *Grinidge, Norwich* is *Noridge, Berwick* is *Berrick*, etc. But this loss of *w* is not consistent; in *Ipswich*, for instance, the second syllable is pronounced *switch*. Am. E. shows similar inconsistencies, though perhaps not quite to the same extent. But note the silent *c* in *Connecticut*, compare *Arkansas* and *Kansas*, and the Fr. sound of *ch* (=*sh*) in *Chicago* and *Michigan* with the normal Eng. sound in *Massachusetts*.

In some groups of words an opposite tendency is shown: Am. E. has a reduced syllable where Br. E. has a full one. This can be seen in several words ending in *–ile*, e.g. *fertile*, which in Br. E. has its second syllable identical with the word *tile*, while Am. E. generally makes the word rime with *Myrtle. Futile, virile, hostile*, etc. sometimes show the same difference. Another example is *record* (noun), in which the second syllable is often slurred in Am. E. but has the same sounds as the word *cord* in Br. E. The

–ine ending fluctuates a good deal; in Br. E. it is usually *–in* or *–een*, as in *genuine* and *quinine* respectively; some American speakers have a "long *i*" in these words or in one of them. Am. E. occasionally has a reduced vowel in the second syllable of *program(me)*, where Br. E. retains a "full" vowel.

Isolated differences in vowel sounds may be noted, such as the vowel in *(n)either*, which is "long *i*" in St. Eng. but often *ee* in Am. E.; Br. E. *tomato*, Am. E. frequently *tomayto*; Br. E. *vahz (vase)*, Am. E. occasionally *vaze* (riming with *haze*) or *vase* (riming with *base*); Br. E. *been* pronounced like *bean*, Am. E. usually *bin*; *patent*, in Am. E. often with the *a* sound of *cat*, in Br. E. *paytent*; *leisure*, Am. E. often *lee–*, in Br. E. riming with *pleasure*; *lever*, in Am. E. often riming with *ever*, Br. E. *leever*.

FORMS AND SYNTAX

Few variations are found in the forms of words as we pass from British to American English. Such as exist are chiefly in the verbs. The verb *dive* has *dived* as its past tense in Br. E., while Am. E. often uses *dove*. Am. E. has a past participle *gotten* as well as *got*, while Br. E. uses *got* alone. But in *forgotten*, *begotten* Br. E. has the *–en* form. Am. E. has *ate* riming with *fate* for the past tense of *eat*, Br. E. has *ate* or *eat*, usually pronounced *et*. The picturesque American forms given by Mencken, such as *brung*, *snuck*, past tense of *bring*, *sneak*, are, one feels, to be looked upon as interesting aberrations; it is unlikely that they will establish themselves in the language, though they are not uncommon in folk-speech and in the comic strip. Am. E. seems to prefer *behoove*, Br. E. *behove*.

A few nouns show slight variations in form, e.g. Am. E. *aLUMinum*, Br. E. *aluMINium*, where both the stress and the ending differ. Am. E. has a singular *inning* (*an inning*) for the word *innings*, where Br. E. would say *an innings*. Am. E. talks about a *raise* in salary, Br. E. a *rise*. British usage on the whole favours *aeroplane*, Amer. *airplane*, Br. E. *cannon* (in billiards), Am. E. *carom*, Br. E. *postcard*, Am. E. *postal card*, Br. E. generally *speciality*, Am. E. *specialty*, Br. E. *recipe*, Am. E. *receipt*. Am. E. uses the form *around* frequently where Br. E. uses *round*, e.g. *He turned round*. According to *Modern English Usage*, *around* is "a disappearing variant of *round*" in Great Britain.

The name of the last letter in the alphabet varies in the two countries; in Great Britain it is *zed*, in Amer. *zee*. The Br. E. form is from the Fr. *zède*, the Am. E. *zee* is on the analogy of *c, t, d, v*, etc.

There are few outstanding syntactic differences between British and American English. A number of features described by Mencken, such as the repeated negative, are equally common among the same class of speakers in England. There is the interesting survival of the genitive in *He works nights*,[7] which is practically unknown in England. The differentiation between *shall* and *will, should* and *would* is not carried out so thoroughly in Am. E. as in St. Eng.; it is chiefly confined to literary style and the speech of the New England seaboard.

The use of *Due to . . .* at the beginning of a clause or sentence is much more common in America than in England and seems to be increasing there. In Br. E. *Owing to . . .* or *Because of . . .* is preferred in this position. An example is Am. E. *Due to the weather the game will not be played*.

A number of variations in the use of prepositions can be observed in the two forms of speech. In England one lives *in* a certain street, in America usually *on* a street. On the other hand Am. E. often has *in* behalf of where Br. E.

7 For the origin of this idiom see p. 68.

has *on* behalf of. Where a British speaker says: There's nothing *in* it an American may say: There's nothing *to* it. Br. E. speaks about: His first holiday *for* four years, Am. E., His first vacation *in* four years, Br. E. a quarter *to* three, Am. E. (often), *of* three. Am. E. tends to use *of* after *all*, e.g. *all of the books*, where Br. E. omits the *of*. A specifically American idiom is the use of *through* meaning "up to and including", e.g. Monday *through* Friday.

Am. E. shows a tendency to use adverbs after verbs, often with an intensifying effect, e.g. *to lose out, to start in, to beat* (*a person*) *up, to back up* (of a vehicle), *to check up on, to slip up* (make a mistake), *to face up to something, to shape up, to tie up with*. This same habit seems, however, to be spreading in Br. E.

There seems to be a tendency in Mod. Amer. literary style to preserve or restore the subjunctive, a form of the verb that had almost vanished. It is often found where Br. E. would use *should*, e.g. Decency required that I *go* to see him. Carol suggested that Miss Sherwin *stay* for supper.[8] This omission of *should* is probably due to a striving for economy in writing rather than a conscious attempt to restore the subjunctive.

Am. E. allows the indefinite *one* to be followed by *his*, a usage that is not normal in Br. E., e.g. *One* does not like to have *his* illusions destroyed. In this sentence most British writers would use *one's* instead of *his*.

Turning to the historical explanation of these divergences between British and American English, we find that many of the American sounds and forms are survivals of older English. Thus, for instance, the unrounded "short *o*" in *not, crop, block* can be traced back to the fifteenth

[8] Quoted from Amer. writers by Jespersen, *Modern English Grammar*; see Stuart Robertson, *British-American Differentiation*, American Speech, Dec. 1939, and C. A. Lloyd, *We Who Speak English*.

century in England[9] and was common in the fashionable speech of the seventeenth and eighteenth centuries, where it can be seen in some of the plays of the period. In Vanbrugh's play *The Relapse* (1696) there is a character, Lord Foppington, later in the next century revived by Sheridan (*A Trip to Scarborough*) who uses words such as *stap, Tam, Gad, bax, pasitively*, etc., for the corresponding words with o. There can be little doubt that this widespread pronunciation was carried over to America by the seventeenth-century colonists and established itself over large areas of this continent, in Canada as well as the U.S.A. In St. Eng. it has died out, and the rounded vowel has persisted in this group of words. This double pronunciation may account for the Eng. forms *Gad* and *strap* by the side of *God* and *strop*.

A similar explanation applies to the "flat *a*" in Amer. *pass, bath, plant*, etc., which also existed in England in the seventeenth century and indeed persists in many English dialects today, but which in St. Eng. has developed into a "broad" *a*.

The survival of a modified *r*-sound in Am. E. in places where it has been lost in St. Eng. (*car, first*, etc.) may well reflect an intermediate stage through which St. Eng. passed before the complete disappearance of the *r*. Some type of *r* sound is still wide-spread, however, in these positions in English folk-speech. American speech may possibly, in this as in other features, follow the St. Eng. tendency and ultimately weaken and drop the *r* in these groups of words.

Earlier forms of English verbs are kept in *dove*, which was originally a strong verb, and *gotten* (cf. *forgotten*), and an earlier function of the genitive is reflected, as we have seen, in the adverbial use of *nights* in such a phrase as *He works nights*. The common Amer. *receipt* (=Br.

[9] See H. C. Wyld, *A History of Colloquial English*, p. 240 ff.

E. *recipe*) is frequently found in eighteenth-century English.

The American syntactical feature of using *one* followed by *his* was not uncommon in earlier English.

14. British and American English: Differences in Vocabulary

British and American English show considerable differences in vocabulary, especially in colloquialisms and groups of technical or semi-technical words. On the literary level, as has been pointed out, the difference is much more slight. These variations are of several types: first, there are words that are not understood on the other side of the Atlantic; second, there are words and expressions that are familiar both to British and American speakers but carry a different meaning or a different range of meaning. The first group consists chiefly of recent slang coinages that have not had time to spread to both countries, or more or less technical words and expressions belonging to a certain trade or profession or to some other activity, such as sports, which has its own specialized vocabulary.

Examples of words which convey no exact meaning to a listener or reader unfamiliar with one or other of these types of English can easily be found. The difficulty arises mainly in the slang expression that is, as it were, self-created, not built up from already existing words. Thus British slang terms such as *wangle* (to obtain by scheming), *scrounge* (a polite term for *steal*), which became popular during World War I (though *wangle* dates back to 1888) or *posh* (luxurious) have not obtained any wide currency in America and would puzzle many American readers, unless their meaning was clearly indicated by the context in which they appear. Similarly American words such as *cahoots, picayune, oodles, hoosegow* would present difficulties to the uninitiated British reader or listener. Other informal expressions, as we shall see, are more self-explanatory and, though possibly strange, set up no serious barrier to communication.

Technical terms which show a similar divergence are numerous. Thus sports and games which belong mainly to one country alone have a vocabulary that is often baffling even to a person in the same country who is not a "fan", and of course still more so to a transatlantic reader. Most cricketing terms, for instance, would puzzle the average American, just as baseball terms are usually unintelligible to the Britisher. How many people in North America could explain what is meant by *"a maiden over"*, and how many Englishmen could interpret a *"two-bagger"*? Other words used in connection with sports would be still more mysterious: the American *bleachers* (open stands, so called presumably because one is bleached in the sun), *rooters* (the vociferous supporters of a team), etc. *Cheer-leader* would explain itself, though the office is unknown in the more sedate British sports, where cheers, if they arise, are spontaneous, and, in the case of the decorous game of cricket, would often be regarded in the same light as brawling in church. In American racing terminology a horse that performs well on soft ground is called "a good *mudder*", a word that does not appear in the English dictionaries. The vocabulary of poker, a game of American origin, is full of terms not immediately understood in England; a number of these, however, have taken on a wider meaning and become colloquialisms in both forms of speech, e.g. *to call a person's bluff*. In fact the word *bluff* has become international and is found in many European languages.

Trades and professions also show divergence in their technical terms. In the academic world America talks of a *campus, credits, units, fields of concentration, flunking,* etc., terms which are not used in Great Britain. Some of these are, however, self-explanatory. In England there are equally mysterious terms, e.g. *don* (tutor at Oxford or Cambridge), *scout, gyp* (College servants at these universities), *quad* (short for *quadrangle*—the nearest equivalent to Amer. *campus,* though not identical)—not to be confused with Eng. *quod,* slang for *jail—tripos, mods, greats* (names of examinations) and other esoteric words. Here too some words are familiar, e.g. *scout,* but are used in a special sense. Student life also has its own special technical vocabulary; the complex terminology surrounding the American fraternity is unknown in England, where this institution does not exist. But the "Public Schools" and older universities have an *argot* of their own or, in fact, each school generally has its own set of traditional terms for its institutions and customs.[1]

The Church also shows a number of terms that differ in Great Britain and America. Both countries have strange sects with names that carry little meaning outside the members of the fold, e.g., Amer. *Jehovah's Witnesses, Holy Rollers, Dunkards,* etc. Even some of the more normal terminology of the English Church may cause difficulty; thus American readers have been puzzled by the expression *"to take holy orders",* and terms such as *vicar, curate, chapter*(*–house*) are not so common in America as in England.

Transport in America and Great Britain shows some interesting differences in terminology. Br. E. *railway* is often Am. E. *railroad;* a *station* may be a *depot,* though *station* is used as well. Many of the variations in railway terms have been explained by the fact that, while the American railroad took over the terminology of the earlier steamboats which were the chief means of public transportation, the British railway system developed from the stage-coach and adopted some of its expressions. This accounts for such

[1] See M. Marples, *Public School Slang.*

nautical terms in Am. E. as *all aboard!*, a *berth*, a *caboose*, originally a place used for cooking on the deck of a ship, then transferred to a freight-train car used by the men in charge, *freight*, originally the cargo of a ship (Am. E. *freight-train* is Br. E. *goods-train*). On the other hand, the Br. E. term *booking-office*, the place at which one buys a ticket for a railway journey, goes back to the days of the stage-coach, when a passenger's name was actually entered in a book and a seat reserved for him. The new procedure in motor-coach travel often makes the word again appropriate. The term *guard* (Am. E. *conductor*) is another relic from the coaching age.[2] Other differences, not due to this cause, are Am. E. *baggage*, Br. E. *luggage*, Am. E. *engineer*, Br. E. *engine-driver*, Am. E. *switch* (verb), Br. E. *shunt*, Am. E. *switch* (noun), Br. E. *points*, Am. E. *tie*, Br. E. *sleeper*, Am. E. *round-trip* (*ticket*), Br. E. *return* (*ticket*), Am. E. *commuter*, Br. E. *season-ticket-holder*, Br. E. *ticket*, Am. E. (occasionally) *transportation*. This use of *transportation* ("I want to buy my *transportation*"), not infrequently heard in America, is an example of a tendency to substitute grandiloquent words that shows itself occasionally in American speech. Another example is *elevator* by the side of the simpler Br. E. *lift*, *funeral director* or *mortician* for *undertaker*, *physician* for *doctor*, *purchase* for *buy*.

Even outside these rather specialized vocabularies different terms may be encountered. Thus what is called in England a *trunk call* is a *long-distance call* in America (here the American term is self-evident, the English term more difficult to interpret), a *draper's shop* (Br. E.) is a *dry-*

---

[2] The use of *boot* as the name of the luggage compartment at the back of a motor-car in England also takes us back to coaching days. Several other terms used in connection with cars differ, e.g., Br. E. *saloon* (*car*) for a closed car, which sounds amusing to Americans, to whom *saloon* usually means Br. E. *public-house* or *local*, *bonnet* for *hood*, *dickey* for *rumble seat*, etc.

goods store (Am. E.), *mineral waters* (Br. E.) are *soft drinks* or *(soda–)pop*, a *pavement* (Br. E.) is a *sidewalk* (here again the American term is less ambiguous), a *chemist's shop* or *chemist's* (Br. E.) is Am. E. *drugstore*, Br. E. *post(man)* is Am. E. *mail(man)*, though Br. E. talks of a *mail-train*, Br. E. *cinema* is Am. E. *movie(s)*, *moving pictures*, Br. E. *draughts*, Am. E. *checkers*, Br. E. *tram(car)*, Am. E. *street-car*, *trolley(–car)*.

Besides these obvious variations in usage there are other cases where the range of meaning in an American word is not the same as in Br. E. One frequently finds that one American term has to do duty for two words in Br. E. denoting two different objects or ideas. An example is *elevator*, which in Am. E. means (1) Br. E. *lift* and (2) a building for storing grain. Similarly, through the common shortening of *gasoline* in everyday speech, the word *gas* now covers in Am. E. the meanings of the two Br. E. words *gas* and *petrol*. *Soda* in Am. E. may mean *washing soda* or an effervescent "soft" drink; the man who dispenses the latter is sometimes called a "soda-jerk". The word *bug* shows a still greater variation in range of meaning: in Am. E. it denotes an insect of almost any kind, in Br. E. one particular variety, the *Cimex lectularius* or bed-bug. It is well for American visitors to England to know this or misunderstandings may easily arise. *Notions* may have the same abstract meaning in Am. E. as in Br. E., but it is also used in the concrete sense of "small, cheap articles of a miscellaneous nature" (buttons, pins, ribbons, etc.), unknown in Br. E. The Br. E. *haberdashery* is the nearest equivalent; in Am. E. *haberdashery*, however, means *male habiliments*. Am. E. *clerk* (pronounced with *er*), covers the meaning of Br. E. *clerk* (pronounced *ar*) and also Br. E. *shop assistant*. Am. E. *store* corresponding to Br. E. *store* (large) and *shop* (small), and Am. E. *shoe* by the side of Br. E. *shoe* (low), *boot* (higher) illustrate a similar tendency. But in some of these terms usage is fluctuating a good deal; *shop*, for instance, is gradually becoming more common in America, while *store* seems to be spreading in Great Britain.

Other parts of speech besides nouns show this same difference. Thus the verb *to ride* is used in Br. E. mainly to refer to riding a horse, in Am. E. to transportation in any kind of vehicle, e.g. a motor-car (where Br. E. would use the word *drive*), train, aeroplane, etc. When this verb becomes a noun it is used in Am. E. to form compounds such as a *boatride* which sound strange to a British ear.

In Br. E. the word *sick*, when used after a verb, e.g. *he is sick*, denotes a condition of nausea (*seasickness*, etc.); for the more general meaning the word *ill* is used. This use of two words, one specialized, the other general, makes for clarity. But before a noun, e.g. *a sick man*, Br. E., like Am. E., uses the word to mean any kind of illness. The wider American connotation of *sick* is, as we shall see, a survival of earlier Eng. usage.

On the other hand, examples may be found of words which in Br. E. carry two meanings for which Am. E. has separate terms. Thus *torch* in Br. E. has the usual old sense of the word and also the more modern meaning of an *electric torch*, called in Am. E. a *flashlight*.

Another kind of difference is seen in a word like *homely*, used in Br. E. in a good sense, in Am. E. in a bad one, a euphemistic substitute for *plain*, *ugly*. To denote the root meaning of *homely* a new American word *homey* has been coined. Here, too, the current American meaning of *homely* is common in earlier English. In the case of the word *guy* the position is, as we have seen, just the opposite; in Am. E. it carries a neutral or a good meaning, in Br. E. a bad one.

Am. E. shows a greater freedom than Br. E. in changing the function of a word without any corresponding change in form, a feature which was characteristic of Elizabethan speech.[3] Thus a noun such as *contact* may become a verb, "to *contact* a person", or may be used as an adjective, "a *contact* man", *suicide* becomes a verb "to *suicide*", as does *railroad*; "to *railroad* a person" is to get rid of him; cf. also "to *railroad* (rush) a measure through the House". The noun *ballyhoo* (originally the sales-talk of a "barker" at a circus) was used as a verb in Mr. Roosevelt's remark (1933): "We cannot *ballyhoo* ourselves into prosperity." A verb may be used as a noun, e.g., "to have another *think* coming"; from the verb *to eat* is formed a noun *eats*, a common sign for roadside refreshment counters, probably developed on the pattern of the noun *drinks*. Even verbs compounded with adverbs are changed in the same way, e.g., a *come-back*, a *get-together*, a *showdown*, a *tie-up*, *shut-ins*, etc. A still more violent change of function is seen in the occasional use of *up* as a verb: "taxes were *upped* (increased)", and *to update* (bring up-to-date). This tendency is especially common in newspaper writing, particularly in headlines where brevity is essential. Thus an investigation is usually called a *probe*, originally a verb, now often used as a noun. It might be noted in passing that this tendency helps to counteract the previously mentioned fondness of Am. E. for long words. *Probe* is more economical than *investigation* and is at the same time a more vivid expression. This accounts for the frequent use of *slay(er)* instead of *murder(er)*, *sleuth* for *detective*, *pact* for *treaty*, etc.

Another direction in which Am. E. shows considerable linguistic enterprise and in which Br. E. is relatively conservative lies in the expansion of endings by attaching them to new words. Thus the suffix *–ician* of *physician*, *musician* has been used to form new words such as *beauti-*

[3] See p. 113.

cian, mortician; –tor has given *realtor* (dealer in real estate); *–eria* (from *cafeteria*) has provided *candyteria, drugeteria, groceteria, foodeteria,* etc.; *–orium* (from *emporium,* etc.) has been used for *crematorium* (also Br.), even (observed in Boston, of all places!) *pantatorium* (dry cleaning and pressing establishment); *–ery* (from *grocery*) has given *bootery, toggery,* etc. The ending *–ize* has been particularly productive in Am. E.—*concertize, hospitalize, institutionalize, picturize, slenderize,* etc. In Br. E. *–drome* has been extended in this way from *hippodrome* to *picturedrome, icedrome.* It is doubtful whether many of these words will obtain wide currency.

The outstanding feature, however, of the modern American vocabulary is the coinage of a large number of expressive colloquial phrases, many of which reveal a high degree of originality and linguistic imagination. The words *highbrow* and *lowbrow* have already been mentioned as examples of this process. These phrases generally consist of a bold, sometimes crude, but vivid metaphor which provides a picturesque and concrete image for an object or an abstract idea. The speaker who invented the term *rubberneck* for an inquisitive person and *rubberneck wagon* for a sightseeing bus, showed considerable linguistic talent. The same is true of *bell-hop* for a page-boy, *carhop, crape-hanger* for a mournful person, *tightwad* for a mean person, *flat tire* for a dull person, *to get cold feet, to deliver the goods,* and the dozen of other American phrases that are so infectious. Their only drawback is, as we have noted, that they are too efficient and soon become irritating through over-use. Then a new term has to be discovered and it too becomes outmoded. The mortality of colloquialisms is very high and their longevity equally low. In a relatively few years, for instance, the expression *to butt in* has been replaced by *to horn in,* and this in its turn superseded by *to chisel in* and *to muscle in;* no doubt the last expression is already on its way out, and a new metaphor, just as ephemeral, will replace it.

Br. E. is, of course, not without its own colloquialisms, some of which are as lively as those of America. Thus two of the ideas mentioned above may be expressed informally in Br. E. quite as effectively: the British equivalent of a *tightwad* is a *skinflint* (in earlier English there were numerous racy words for a miserly person, e.g., *nipcheese*), and a mournful person is a *wet blanket*. But often the American term conveys an idea more directly. Thus the American *movie(s)* is more vivid than the British *cinema*, which does not reflect the idea of a moving as opposed to a static picture. At a lower level Br. has "the flicks" or "a flick", which presents a different image. When Aldous Huxley in *Brave New World* had to coin a new term for his prophetic new film in the remote future which will enable the audience, if they wish, to experience the sensations of the players on the screen, he used the word *feelies*, modelled on *movies*. On the other hand, to be quite just, one should point out that the British term *wireless* does contain a definite idea that is not seen in the American *radio*, which, like *cinema*, short for earlier *oinematograph*, is an abbreviation of *radio-telegraph*. Am. E., however, uses *wireless* in connection with telegraphic or telephonic communication. Other British slang expressions which have the vividness of American speech are *to get the wind up* (to be nervous), a product of World War I, *to pull one's leg*, a *leg-pull* (to fool a person). But much British slang is of the rather arbitrary type such as the previously quoted *scrounge, wangle, posh*. And when we find distinguished British statesmen and writers using American slang in their books and public utterances it is certainly a tribute to these racy expressions as a means of communication. Thus Monsignor R. A. Knox, a typical product of Oxford, in a book which breathes the spirit of that ancient seat of learning

(*Let Dons Delight*) made his dons talk about a *come-back* and a *wise-crack*. The habit has spread even to France. Premier Paul Reynaud, broadcasting to America in April, 1940, said that the French would not accept a "phoney" peace. The popularity of these American phrases, especially in the propaganda age, is no doubt partly due to a consideration of their effect on the transatlantic audience. It might be noted that British orators and writers often get their Americanisms wrong. Thus Mr. Chamberlain, in a post-Munich speech, after explaining that the Americans had a phrase a *go-getter*, proceeded to use it in an unidiomatic way; he said he was a *go-getter for peace*. The American phrase "*I am* (*he is*) *a go-getter*" is complete; one would not normally say "a go-getter for something". And Sir Samuel Hoare, in his famous "jitterbug" speech, showed that he completely misunderstood the meaning of this term, confusing it, not unnaturally, with the phrase "the jitters". When he said that the British people were not jitterbugs, he did not realize that the word meant persons who cannot resist "swing" music or "hot" music of any kind and feel compelled to get up and dance to it; he intended of course to say that the British were not afraid, i.e., were not "jittery" or "did not have the jitters". But it is not surprising to find that, in following the complexities of the European situation, political leaders sometimes fail to keep quite abreast of American slang. On the other hand, one is startled to find so careful and conscientious a craftsman as Galsworthy putting into the mouth of an American character in his play *The Little Man* phrases that surely no American ever uses. A few examples are: *Get a wiggle on you!* (Hurry up!), *I shall admire* (be surprised), *What do you opine?*, *Oh, Sir!*, *Yep!*, *How did it eventuate* (happen)?, *That's quite an indisposition* (illness), *You don't suspicion* (suspect), *That's where you slop over* (make a mistake), *a sure-enough saint*. This is

American speech as seen through British eyes. No doubt American writers attempting British slang make equally glaring mistakes. The moral is, that if a writer or speaker has to use colloquialisms from the other side of the Atlantic, he ought to get a native to test their accuracy.

HISTORICAL ORIGIN OF AMERICANISMS

These special features of the American vocabulary originate in various ways. Some, like similar phenomena in American pronunciation, are survivals of earlier English words or meanings; others represent loan-words from the foreign languages that have been or still are spoken on the American continent; others are American-built coinages from English speech-material; finally, there are a few original words created on American soil.

American Survivals from Earlier English

The first group, words or meanings surviving from earlier English, is probably not so large as some writers on American English have suggested. From time to time attempts are made to prove that Am. E. is really Elizabethan English; this obviously is going too far. When, for instance, we find Shakespeare using *Let me tell the world* in somewhat the same sense as the modern American *I'll tell the world* or *You have said* with about the same meaning as Am. E. *You said it*, it is not safe to assume that the two modern phrases are directly descended from Elizabethan English. There is always the possibility that they arose independently in recent times. On the other hand, there is a stronger claim in the case of the expression *I guess*, used by Chaucer in exactly the same sense as in Modern Am. E.

> Of twenty yeer of age he was, I *gesse*.
> (I guess he was about twenty.)

This is found in English down to the seventeenth century and even later, and may quite well be the ancestor of the present-day Americanism, which is gradually being introduced into England once more. Nor can we doubt that the American use of the word *deck* to mean a pack of cards is a survival when we read in Shakespeare (3 Henry VI, V, 1, 43)

> But, whiles he thought to steal the single ten,
> The king was slily finger'd from the *deck*.

And *homely* in the sense of *plain, ugly* is well established in earlier English, as can be seen from the quotation from 1612 recorded in the *Shorter Oxford Dictionary*: "Some parts of Man . . . be *comely*, some *homely*." *Sick* in the general sense of *ill* is also frequent in older English, e.g., in biblical language. The American use of *mad* in the sense of *angry* goes back to earlier English: cf. Psalm 102, 8: "They that are *mad* against me are sworn against me." In Mod. E. *mad* usually means *insane* (=Am. E. *crazy*). *Fall* for *autumn* is another instance; it is still used occasionally as a poetical word in Br. E., but the normal word is *autumn*. It is curious that this one word of French origin should have found its way into the names of the seasons, all of which were originally native English words. In Am. E. the group preserves its homogeneous character: *spring, summer, fall, winter*. *Fall* is of course a shortening for *the fall of the leaf*. The word *chore(s)* is an interesting example of a word that has died out completely in Br. E., except perhaps in dialect, where many of these older forms persist, but which is very common in Am. E., particularly in the rural districts. In Br. E. it can still be seen as the first element of *char-*

woman; it is connected with O.E. *cierran*, "to turn". But, in relation to the total vocabulary, the number of these survivals is not very large.

Loan-Words in American English

The loan-words introduced into Am. E. through contact with foreign languages on this continent form an interesting collection; as usual, they reflect the kind of influence exerted by one culture on another. The earliest instances of this infiltration are the American Indian words. The largest group of these consists no doubt of the numerous geographical names taken over from the Indians, often in a more or less distorted form. The map of North America is abundantly strewn with these relics of an older civilization. They are far more picturesque, when translated into English, than the ordinary name of British origin, and still more so than some of the rather ugly or pretentious modern American geographical names. Mississippi (=Big River) is superior, in sound, appearance and meaning, to Bloggsville, Jones's Corners or Enterprise. Ottawa took a wise step in restoring its ancient Indian name and substituting it for the commonplace Bytown. It is not surprising that Alabama is a constant inspiration for lyrics and Niagara a mecca for honeymooners. On the other hand, there are Skowhegan, Skaneateles, Kalamazoo and Saskatchewan, which are not so euphonious.

Besides place-names a number of ordinary words have been adopted from the Indian languages. Many of these have penetrated into Br. E., mainly through the medium of "redskin" literature. Examples are *squaw, tomahawk, wigwam, pow-wow, moccasin, papoose,* all of which carry with them an atmosphere of adventure and romance. Other expressions associated with Indian life but built up from English speech-material, perhaps in some cases translations of Indian terms, are *paleface, redskin, to scalp, medicine man, fire-water*. The Indian equivalent of *fire-water* is *hooch*, a term that enjoyed a certain popularity during the age of prohibition.

Terms with less exciting connotations are borrowed to denote natural objects such as *skunk, squash* (a gourd—Ind. *asquutasquash*), *hickory, persimmon, cayuse, opossum, moose, chipmunk*.[4] Some of these are familiar to English readers, others not. *Mugwump,* an Indian term meaning "great chief", has been transferred to Am. E. in the sense of a political boss, especially one who remains independent of a party. *Sachem,* another term for an Indian chief, has also taken on a political significance.

French, Spanish, Dutch and German have also contributed words to Am. E., as the American settlers in various regions were in close contact with speakers of these languages. From Fr. are derived such words as *cent, dime, chowder* (a soup—cf. Fr. *chaudière,* a pot), *portage, cache, levee* (an embankment), certain geographical terms such as *prairie, butte* (isolated hill), *bayou* (marshy portions of lakes and rivers), probably *shanty, caribou* (the latter, according to the *S.O.D.,* from Canadian Fr.). The name of the fish *gaspereau,* common in Nova Scotia, seems to be Fr. It is also called the *alewife.* The word *pumpkin* is a Fr. word with an interesting history. It was originally a Fr. loan-word in England and appears in earlier English as *pompion* or *pumpion,* referring sometimes to a big man, e.g., applied in Shakespeare's *Merry Wives of Windsor* to Falstaff: "this unwholesome humidity, this gross watery *pumpion.* . . ." (III, 3, 43). Then it was changed to *pumpkin,* probably by popular etymology. The new form *pumpkin* (Am. E. often *punkin*) is recorded, according to

---

[4] According to the *S.O.D.,* this may possibly be an English compound.

the S.O.D., from 1647, and a slang use to indicate a puffed-up, self-important person from 1848. An interesting Fr. loan-word which survives in many American rural dialects is *shivaree*, the term applied to the noisy and boisterous celebration sometimes staged outside the house of a newly-married couple; it is derived from Fr. *charivari*, with the same meaning, a word also used as a sub-title for *Punch* (the London *Charivari*). In modern times Am. E. has coined certain "synthetic" Fr. expressions such as *pie-à-la-mode*.

From Sp. a number of words have been borrowed, a large proportion of which are connected in one way and another with horses and riding, reflecting one of the major activities of the Spanish west and south. The term *cinch* is an interesting example; originally it meant a saddle-girth, then, because this had to be fixed tightly, it developed the sense of a "firm hold", a "dead certainty", a "sure thing" and even "something easy". It can even be used as a verb with various meanings such as "to get a sure hold of". *Rodeo* is another of these Sp. terms, first meaning a cattle round-up, then a cowboy exhibition, and then applied to other types of entertainments, e.g., *a motorcycle rodeo*; its accent is generally placed one syllable earlier than in the original Sp. pronunciation. Other words in this category are *chaps*, an abbreviation of *chaperejos* (Mexican Sp.), *sombrero*, *bronc(h)o* (from a Sp. word meaning *rough*, *rude*), *stampede*, *lariat*, *lasso*, *barbecue*, and possibly *quirt* (a whip). The *gallon* in a *ten-gallon hat* is from a Sp. word *galón* meaning *braid*, used as the trimming for a hat. The change to *gallon* is due to popular etymology. *Galloon*, from the Fr. form of this word, is found in Eng. in the seventeenth century.[5] *Hoosegow* and *calaboose*, two words for jail, are from Sp., as are two other associated terms, *incommunicado* and *vigilantes*.

---

[5] See *American Speech*, Oct. 1939 and S.O.D. under *galloon*.

Lagniappe, something given as a present when a purchase is made, and *savannah*, a treeless plain, a geographical term not infrequent in Nova Scotia, are from the same language. *Carom* (at billiards) is derived ultimately from Sp. *carambola*. *Cuspidor*, an American "elegant variation" for *spittoon*, is of Portuguese origin. It will be seen that the Sp. ingredient in the American vocabulary is of a rather romantic and picturesque character. It raises in our minds images of frontier adventure and the atmosphere of the "western". Some of these terms, such as *stampede*, *bronco*, are familiar to British readers, others such as *hoosegow*, *calaboose* would need explanation.

The Du. and Ger. element is less romantic. From the period of the Dutch settlements along the Hudson and in other parts of the U.S. and Canada a number of words have been adopted from this language. They include a group of words for articles of food such as *cookie*, *waffle*, *cruller* (a hole-less doughnut), *cole-slaw* (salad made of cabbage), sometimes changed by popular etymology to *cold-slaw*. There are also miscellaneous words like *stoop*, a platform attached to a house, *corral* (cf. Du. *kraal*), *snoop* (to pry), *boss*, *log(e)y* (dull, heavy) and also possibly *pit* (of a cherry). The term *Santa Claus* is an American creation from Du. dialect *Sante Klaas* (=Saint Nicholas). *Filibuster* is a curious mixture of a Du. word, originally the same word as *freebooter*, and Sp. *filibustero*. Its use in the sense of one who practises sustained obstruction in a legislature is purely American. *Dope*, a term of Du. origin, provides a good illustration of the ramifications of a word in colloquial American speech. Derived from a Du. verb cognate with Eng. *dip*, it meant first a thick liquid, then perhaps because of its similarity to the first part of *opium*, it was used to denote a preparation for doctoring horses, then any kind of narcotic (cf. *dope-fiend*). It may also mean information, and, as a verb, *to dope out*, to collect information and work out a problem or assignment. Recently an adjective *dopey* has been formed with the meaning stupid, and *dope* can also be used as a noun to indicate a stupid person. One who hands out information may be called a *dopester*.[6] *Dope* and *fix* are two of the most useful words in the American vocabulary; they can be employed to cover a great many situations. Some of these Du. words have passed over from Am. E. into Br. E.

Ger. has also provided a number of words mainly connected with eating and drinking, e.g., *delicatessen* (originally from Fr.), *sauerkraut, pretzel, weiner, hamburger* (these two terms probably American shortenings of longer Ger. compounds, e.g., *Wienerwurst*), *rathskeller, lager, bock*, etc. *Hamburger* has given rise, through the extension of the suffix *-burger* and the erroneous identification of the first syllable with the word *ham*, to a large number of new coinages such as *chickenburger, cheeseburger*, even *nutburger* and *bananaburger*. The American slang term *kibitzer* (an onlooker at a card game) may be derived from Ger. *kiebitz*, "a lapwing, peewit", suggesting the idea of the watcher hovering over the table. Another slang term from Ger. is *spiel*, and *nix* (no) may be a distortion of Ger. *nicht(s)*. *Bund*, "league, union", has been introduced through the activity of the German-American Bund. It is possible that the current Amer. use of *dumb* in the sense of stupid, *fresh* (=impudent) and *bum* (=a tramp) is due to the influence of similar Ger. words. Here again Br. E. has taken over such terms as *delicatessen, lager*, while *kibitz(er)* would sound exotic and baffling. *Bum*, with a different origin and meaning, is mildly obscene in Br. E., and a slight shudder goes through a British movie audience when one of the characters in an American picture calls another "a dirty bum".

6 For *Santa Claus, filibuster* and *dope* see S.O.D.

The various other processes of word-creation seen in Br. E. can also be observed in Am. E. Thus we have examples of American words coined from proper names in *maverick*, a term applied to young, unbranded cattle and taken from the name of Samuel Maverick, who owned such cattle in Texas in the 'forties. It is used in a transferred sense to denote a roving, masterless young person. *Tuxedo*, the American term for a dinner-jacket, is named after a club, which in its turn takes its name from a place, Tuxedo Park, New York. Echoic Amer. words are seen in *blizzard*, *zip(per)*, *wow*, *oomph*; terms coined by individual writers are *blurb* and *booboisie*, the latter a "blend" of *boob* (a stupid person) and *bourgeoisie*. A number of American words are of obscure origin, and their derivation still has to be discovered; examples are *jitney*, *jazz*, *hoodlum*, *picayune*, and the term *Yankee*, for which many explanations have been proposed, none of which is quite convincing.

The greater number of American innovations in the vocabulary are constructed from English speech-material. The borrowing of foreign words has not been extensive; naturally, as it is spread over a period of little more than three centuries, it cannot be compared with the vast number of loan-words which at various periods have entered the language of Great Britain. And for the same reason the newly created words do not constitute a large proportion of the total vocabulary. These American coinages from English material, which have already been illustrated and of which many more examples could be given, present no barrier, as a rule, to adoption in Great Britain. Unlike some of the foreign and created words, their meaning is self-evident or can usually be easily guessed; they contain a novel and often arresting combination of current English words. This accounts for the ease with which they circulate in Great Britain, especially since the arrival of the radio, TV, and the film has facilitated their journey across the Atlantic and introduced them directly to millions of British people.

This fact enables us to answer the last two closely connected questions formulated above: Are the differences between Br. E. and Am. E. increasing or decreasing, and are these differences of such a nature as to justify the term, "the American language"? Improved means of communication, the direct presentation of American speech to vast numbers of British listeners and the similar exposure of American audiences to Br. E. through the medium of the B.B.C., British films, and frequently even American films with British actors and actresses, or Americans who have acquired an English accent, the presence, during and since the war of numerous American servicemen and their families in Britain, all these factors are bound to familiarize the two countries with each other's form of English, and, while not necessarily bringing about uniformity, will at least tend to prevent further divergence. And this is a cumulative process; as time goes on the mutual influence of the two types of speech will increase. It is conceivable that a "mid-Atlantic" compromise dialect may develop in due course, but it is dangerous to prophesy with regard to language. Of one thing we may, however, be sure: Noah Webster's prediction, quoted above, that Br. E. and Am. E. would ultimately become mutually unintelligible is, like so many guesses about linguistic developments, highly improbable.

From the British side many signs of greater tolerance, even of enthusiasm, for so-called Americanisms can be detected. Instances of eminent public men deliberately using transatlantic phrases have already been given. Two pronouncements, one by an author who died some years ago, the other by a distinguished novelist, may be adduced in evidence. First we may cite William Archer, a prominent dramatic critic, who wrote in 1921:

"The current English of today owes a great deal to America, and though certain American writers carry to excess the cult of slang, that tendency is not the least affecting serious American literature and journalism. Much of the best and purest English of our time has been, and is being, written in America. . . . If English journalists make a show of arrogant and self-righteous Briticism, it is quite possible that a certain class of American journalists may retaliate by setting afoot a deliberately anti-British movement and attempting (as an American has wittily put it) to 'deserve well of mankind by making two languages grow where only one grew before.' "[7]

In 1925 the well-known novelist, Virginia Woolf, was even more enthusiastic in her praise. "For the Americans are doing what the Elizabethans did—they are coining new words. They are instinctively making their language adapt itself to their needs. In England, save for the impetus given by the war, the word-coining power has lapsed —our writers vary the metres of their poetry, remodel the rhythm of prose, but one may search English fiction in vain for a single new word.[8] It is significant that when we want to freshen our speech we borrow from America— *poppycock, rambunctious, booster, good-mixer*—all the expressive, ugly, vigorous slang which creeps into use among us, first in talk, later in writing, comes from across the Atlantic. Nor does it need much foresight to predict that

[7] Quoted by H. L. Mencken (*The American Language*) from an article in the *Westminster Gazette*.
[8] There is perhaps a little exaggeration here. James Joyce, for instance, coined a good many words, some of which he alone seemed to understand. But Joyce was an Irish expatriate.

when words are being made a literature will be made out of them."[9]

In the light of statements such as these, of which many more could be quoted, it is obvious that the antagonism to American forms of speech which previously existed in certain quarters in Great Britain is rapidly dying out. Not all Americanisms are received with equal favour; there is naturally a selective process, which rejects certain neologisms either because they are not needed or because they make no appeal. But the attitude that condemns a new expression simply because it originates on the other side of the Atlantic, without any consideration of its usefulness as an addition to the language, is now largely confined to purists and the linguistic die-hard who is a victim of his prejudices. Among the young and those who are alert to new developments in language there is a welcome for innovations that fill a gap in our linguistic material or have the merit of freshness and novelty. The skilful writer or speaker maintains a nicely adjusted balance between orthodoxy and experiment. And this is in line, as we have seen, with the whole tradition of English, which has, throughout its long history, absorbed new words and phrases without regard to their origin. In the course of time almost every source has been drawn upon to enlarge the boundaries of our English speech, and the result is the wonderful copiousness of our vocabulary and its capacity to convey the most delicate shades of meaning and produce the most varied emotional effects. If America can contribute to the ever-expanding resources of the English tongue her gifts ought certainly to be welcome.

There is thus no real basis for a claim to an independent American language. The literary language shows no essential differences in the two countries. Popular speech

[9] Quoted from an article in the *Saturday Review of Literature*.

has a little more divergence, but not nearly so much as might be imagined, and in the one field where the variations are most striking, that of vocabulary, they are not sufficient to justify the term "the American Language".

15. Recording Present-Day Speech

In the first chapter of this book emphasis was laid on the continuous process of change that can be detected in any language that is still spoken as a living tongue. Some of the changes and developments in English have been illustrated in the chapters that followed. We noted also that, in response to new needs and trends, our language is still being modified. It is a tempting but dangerous task to try to prophesy its future path. Any such prediction, which is almost sure to be wrong, ought to be based partly on past tendencies in the history of English and other languages, and partly on the forces that are in operation at the present time. It is important, therefore, for this purpose and for other reasons, to have a clear idea of the types of English used today by speakers of various generations, localities and social classes.

The systematic study of the speech-habits of groups of people in different regions of a country has been pursued actively in recent times. It is a comparatively new subject, generally known as linguistic geography. In various European countries maps have been drawn up which chart important features in the language. These are combined into a linguistic atlas, and such atlases are in existence or are being prepared for about twenty different countries. Besides providing a clear picture of interesting linguistic phenomena, these maps are useful to the historian and the ethnologist because they throw light on certain racial groupings and on conditions of early settlement and movements of population in different regions. They show how communities have spread in various directions from one centre, taking with them characteristic features of their speech. They are also of interest to the sociologist because of the information they yield about the speech-pattern of different age-groups and different social strata in the population. We can learn from a study of this material some of the dominant trends in everyday speech. Such information should be of interest to the speech-reformer; he will be better equipped for the task of improving standards of speech, if he is able to recognize the prevailing tendencies in the language of his locality and to adjust his methods and aims in the light of these discoveries; it is of little use attempting to impose on a community a new type of speech unrelated or in opposition to that which already exists. Much enthusiasm and energy is wasted by speech-missionaries because this is not recognized. Finally, the student of the history of a language will also benefit from the study of the results of these investigations; he will be able to observe older forms that have survived in local varieties of speech and to detect tendencies parallel to those that have been at work in past stages of the language.

This material can best be collected in relatively isolated communities, whose speech has not been exposed too much to the levelling influence of education, the radio, television, and the film, and whose members have not travelled far from their native place. Under these circumstances linguistic trends show themselves more clearly, and natural processes can operate more fully; thus a more clear-cut picture of speech can be obtained than, for instance, in a large city with a population of very mixed origin. But for a complete account of a language all types of speakers must of course ultimately be included, old and young, urban and rural, cultured and uncultured.

Linguistic maps were first made in France and Germany. The French *Atlas linguistique* of Gillieron and Edmont and the German *Sprachatlas des deutschen Reiches*, inaugurated by Wenker and continued by Wrede, were the pioneer works of this type. Other continental countries and parts of countries gradually followed: Switzerland, Italy, part of Spain, the Scandinavian lands, and so on. The English-speaking countries were very late in undertaking this enquiry. A pioneer project in England is the *Survey of English Dialects*, by Harold Orton and Eugen Dieth, which is in course of preparation. A number of detailed studies of isolated dialects have been made, mostly by non-English scholars, and a large amount of information about dialects is also contained in Joseph Wright's monumental *English Dialect Dictionary* and his *Dialect Grammar*. But it is obvious that dialect forms entered alphabetically in a dictionary cannot present a picture of human speech and its distribution as clearly as a series of maps.

In 1928, a scheme was launched to chart the speech of North America—the *Linguistic Atlas of the United States and Canada*. This is a large-scale project, a part of which has already been completed. Over six hundred maps have been drawn up showing features of New England speech, and a *Handbook* has been published dealing with the methods, some of the results, and the historical background of this work.[1] This is only the first instalment—a very small fraction—of a comprehensive scheme that will ultimately cover the whole of the North American continent; further work is in progress in other regions of the United States and Canada.

The first problem in a survey of this kind is to select suitable communities where the conditions are favourable for the preservation of a genuine local type of speech.

[1] *Linguistic Atlas of New England; Handbook of the Linguistic Geography of New England.*

This can best be done by a historian who is familiar with the conditions of early settlements and the subsequent history of the region. The most fruitful localities are generally somewhat off the beaten track, if possible remote from highways, railroads and large centres of population. In these places suitable informants are chosen, usually speakers who have not travelled a great deal, some old, some middle-aged or young, representing various social strata; thus a cross-section of the speech of the community is obtained. The language of one or two typical speakers is then recorded by means of a questionnaire, originally containing about 900 items, now generally reduced to about 500. These questions cover almost every aspect of everyday life, as can be seen from some of the headings: *the weather; parts of the house and farm; utensils, implements, vehicles; clothing and bedding; topography, roads; domestic and other animals; food, cooking, meals; trees, berries; parts of the body; personal characteristics; emotions; illnesses; death; social life and institutions; religion, superstitions.* The answers, obtained, if possible, not by direct questioning but in the course of ordinary conversation, are written down in a phonetic alphabet which indicates the exact sounds used. Samples of speech recorded in this way are taken in a large number of communities—in the more settled parts of New England about every fifteen miles, in more sparsely settled districts at greater intervals—and the results collated and entered on maps. A separate map is used for each of the several hundred items investigated. The form heard at a certain place is entered on the outline map, and thus the complete picture is built up for the whole region under investigation. Some of these maps will be important mainly for lexical variants, i.e. they will show a large number of different words for the same object or idea, others will show differences in pronunciation of the same word or words, others features of syntax, and others differences in the meaning of the same word. By the use of symbols a more definite idea of the distribution of any one feature can be obtained. Thus the diagram below shows the distribution of certain terms for *cottage cheese* in New England. This is not a complete picture of *all* the terms used, but merely a selection to illustrate the existence of speech-belts based on the occurrence of four different words. This is a lexical map. The second chart shows the

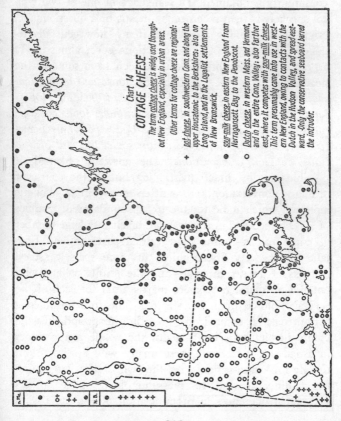

Chart 14
COTTAGE CHEESE

The term <u>cottage cheese</u> is widely used throughout New England, especially in urban areas.

Other terms for cottage cheese are regional:

<u>pot cheese</u>, in southwestern Conn. and along the upper Housatonic to the Berkshires; also on Long Island and in the Loyalist settlements of New Brunswick.

<u>sour-milk cheese</u>, in eastern New England from Narragansett Bay to the Penobscot.

<u>Dutch cheese</u>, in western Mass. and Vermont, and in the entire Conn. Valley; also farther east, where it competes with sour-milk cheese. This term presumably came into use in western New England, owing to contacts with the Dutch in the Hudson Valley, and spread eastward. Only the conservative seaboard barred the intruder.

distribution of the "broad *a*" and the "flat *a*" in a group of words.[2] These are only two out of several hundred examples of the way in which information about speech-habits is recorded; such investigations clearly reflect the facts of North American speech. They will throw light on a large number of much-debated questions about usage.

Even at this early stage of the enquiry many interest-

[2] These charts are reproduced by kind permission of the *Linguistic Atlas.*

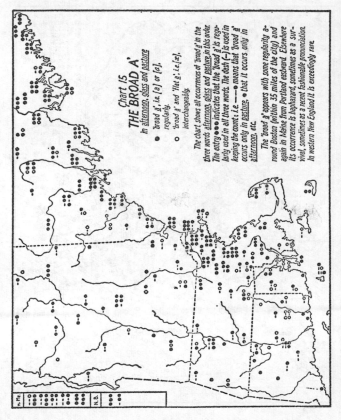

Chart 15
THE BROAD A'
in *afternoon, glass* and *pasture*

● 'broad *a*', i.e. [a] or [ɑ], regularly.

○ 'broad *a*' and 'flat *a*', i.e. [æ], interchangeably.

The chart shows all occurrences of 'broad *a*' in the three words *afternoon, glass* and *pasture* in this order. The entry ●●● indicates that the 'broad *a*' is regularly used in all three words. The dash (—) is used in keeping the count; i.e. ──● means that 'broad *a*' occurs only in *pasture*. ●── that it occurs only in *afternoon,* etc.

The 'broad *a*' appears with some regularity around Boston (within 35 miles of the city) and again in Maine from Portland eastward. Elsewhere its occurrence is haphazard, sometimes as a survival, sometimes as a recent fashionable pronunciation. In western New England it is exceedingly rare.

VII. 5. 11. SNACK (between breakfast and the midday meal)

Do you have anything to eat between meals?

- ● BAGGING
- ○ BAIT
- ◓ BEAVER
- ⟂ BITING-ON
- ⊤ BREAKS
- ◔ CLOCKING
- ◉ COFFEE-TIME
- ◑ CRIB
- ◯ CRUST
- ◌ DEW-BIT
- ◖ DOCKY
- ◗ DOWEN
- ◴ DRINKING
- ♪ DRUM-UP
- ◢ (E)LEVENSES
- //// FORENOON DRINKING
- ⋀ FORENOONS
- ◬ JOWER
- ◭ LOWANCE
- ▢ LUNCH
- ◀ MINNING-ON
- ✕ NAMMET
- ✳ NAMMETS
- ✼ NAMMICK
- ◈ NINESES
- ✺ NUMMET
- ✻ NUMMICK
- ✕ NUNCH
- ✗ NUNCHEON
- → PROGGER
- ⊤ PUTTING-ON
- ◹ SANDWICHES
- ◼ SNACK
- ▼ SNACK-BIT
- ◤ SNECK
- ▣ SNAP
- ▦ SNAPPING
- ⚘ SUP AND A BITE
- ◰ TEN O CLOCK
- ⋔ TENNER
- ⋀⋀ TENSES

LINGUISTIC ATLAS OF ENGLAND

(DRAFT MAP)

ing features have emerged. First, as one might expect, many speakers are to a certain extent bilingual; they have a double standard in their speech, one type being used in ordinary spontaneous conversation, another when on their guard. Thus a husband, when asked directly how he would refer to his wife, will answer: "I call her *Mrs. X*"; a few minutes later he will refer to her quite naturally as "the (my) wife" or, at a certain social level and in certain localities, "the woman". Similar examples of a double usage are found in the names of male animals, for which in everyday speech among men the ordinary words are employed—*bull, ram,* etc.—but which are often replaced, among women or among men when women are present, by euphemistic substitutes of the type mentioned in Chapter 10.

Secondly, numerous instances of forms and meanings current in earlier English appear in the local dialects, which thus throw light on the history of the language. This applies not only to vocabulary but also to pronunciation and syntax. Thus older speakers may talk of a *waistcoat* (often pronounced *weskit*), *wristbands* (cuffs), *the chamber* (=the bedroom or else the whole upper floor of a house), *tempest* (storm), *buttery* (pantry), *grandsir* or *grandther* (grandfather), etc., words which were previously normal parts of the vocabulary. *Weskit* also illustrates the survival of an older pronunciation of an unstressed syllable; a similar reduction is seen in *fortnit* (fortnight); in these, as in many other words, the standard language has restored the "full" vowel in the ending. *Mistress* for *Mrs.* (misiz) shows the older form of this word before the sounds *tr* were dropped; it can still be heard in certain parts of Nova Scotia. *Deef* for *deaf* is a relic of an earlier pronunciation of this word, in which the development is exactly parallel to *leaf*. *Sassengers* for *sausages* shows an insertion of *n* which, as we have seen, is similar to what has happened in the words *passenger,* *messenger.* The common dialectal pronunciation of *hearth* with the same vowel as *earth* represents an earlier stage in the history of this word, while the occasional use of *varmint* (developed from *vermin*) with *ar* shows an opposite tendency and also the insertion of a final *–t* parallel to that of *against* and other words.

Many relics can be seen in the verbs, though they are gradually being displaced by the standard forms. Thus the verb *climb,* instead of following the weak pattern with a past tense *olimbed,* a development of the modern period, sometimes shows its original strong past in the form *clum(b),* i.e. it is parallel to *wring, wrung.* This is historically a more genuine form than *climbed.* Similarly *catched* is an older form which existed before it was replaced by *caught;* it too is often preserved in regional dialects. In the strong verbs interesting historical forms occur; the dialectal *riz* (the sun *riz*) can be traced back to Middle English as an alternative to *rose,* which has established itself as the normal form; *driv,* which may be heard instead of *drove,* is exactly parallel. Both forms are derived from the M.E. plural of the past tense; they are analogous to *bite, bit.*

As an example of the survival of an older meaning one might mention the wide-spread use of the word *clever* in New England and Nova Scotia in the sense of *generous, hospitable,* etc. In the eighteenth century we find it in English with exactly the same signification, e.g. in Goldsmith's *She Stoops to Conquer:*

> Then come, put the jorum about
> And let us be merry and *clever.*

Technical terms from certain occupations are occasionally transferred to ordinary speech, a process already illustrated in Chapter 11. Thus in a community on the seaboard, where the language of the sea exerts a considerable influence, the expression "I ran afoul of him" is often used to denote an accidental meeting, not necessarily of an unpleasant nature. Terms describing the winds and the weather frequently show a special nautical colouring in these localities. Another phrase which seems to have been introduced either from the language of the vessels or perhaps of lumbering camps is a "mug-up", heard instead of the more usual *snack, lunch* or *bite*.

Interesting results of a mixture of languages can also be detected. In certain regions of the United States and Canada the so-called "Dutch" (often really German) influence is marked, especially in parts of Pennsylvania, Ontario, and the Lunenberg district of Nova Scotia. This is reflected both in pronunciation and idiom, e.g. the frequent substitution, among older speakers, of *d* and *t* for the two sounds of *th* as in *then* and *thin*, a "uvular" *r* for the normal *r*-sound in *red*, etc. Picturesque constructions, not heard in the standard language, may be due to the carrying-over of a non-English idiom, e.g. "tik (thick) of fog" (=very foggy), "Are you coming with?", "The cat's wanting out." The last phrase may, however, be a relic of an earlier English practice, since a verb indicating motion is, as we have seen, frequently omitted in older stages of the language. The calls to animals, which form an interesting part of such a survey, show variation in these regions of mixed speech; the pig, for instance, is often called with the words *woots, woots, woots* or *wootsh, wootsh, wootsh*.

Among the Gaelic-speaking inhabitants of Nova Scotia a similar influence of non-English speech-habits can be detected. Such speakers often have difficulty in pronouncing the "voiced" sounds of *v, z,* etc., and substitute for them the corresponding "breathed" sounds *f, s,* etc. They too carry words over from their original Gaelic idiom, e.g. *loft* used in the sense of "the upper part of a house", a meaning which the Gaelic *lobht* has in addition to the more usual one. Some of the animal calls are derived from Gaelic; the sheep are often called with the words *kiry, kiry, kiry* or (approximately) *kirsh, kirsh, kirsh*; compare the Gaelic words for sheep, *caor(a)* and *caorach, caoirich*, etc.

The variety of terms used to denote various objects, processes and ideas is striking. Here are a few examples. No less than twenty-one expressions have been recorded in New England for the *earthworm* and are shown on the complete map for this item (*Linguistic Atlas of New England*, vol. 1, Map 236). Some of them are *angleworm* (the most common term), *angledog, angler, groundworm, dirtworm, muckworm, eelworm, rainworm* and also more picturesque and descriptive names such as *nightwalker, nightprowler, nightcrawler*.

A similar range is seen in the expressions for the *seesaw*, which changes its name frequently from one locality to another. The most common term in New England is *teeter* or some variant of this: *teeter board, teenter, tinter, teetle-(board)*, etc. But in certain regions, especially in and near Cape Cod, *tilt, tiltin board* and *tilter* are found. *Tilter* seems to be a "blend" of *tilt* and *teeter*. There are also quite different expressions such as *dandle* and *dandle board* and the picturesque *tippety-bounce*. The word *seesaw* itself is also generally known, but is often felt to be somewhat literary.[3] In Nova Scotia most of these words are heard and in addition *tippin board* and *sawman*. It is interesting to note that the form *teeter-totter*, which is very common in Ontario, is rare in New England and Nova Scotia.

The noisy and riotous celebration that is sometimes staged in certain localities after a marriage, when the

[3] See H. Kurath, *New England Words for the Seesaw*, American Speech, April, 1933.

neighbours of the newly-married couple gather outside the house and blow horns, beat tin cans, ring cowbells and fire guns, usually continuing until they are treated to something to eat and drink—a honeymoon racket—has an equally large variety of names to describe it. The most wide-spread term in New England is the *serenade*, but there are also many others. A few are *callathump(in), rouser, bellin, saluting, celebration, tin-panning, tin pan shower, horning*.[4] *Shivaree* is also very common in certain districts; the origin of this word has already been discussed. Most of these terms are also heard in Nova Scotia, though the practice seems to be dying out. One of the most interesting variants for this ritual is the term *skimmelton* (also *skimmerton, skimmiton*); this word existed in earlier English and is used in one of the closing chapters of Thomas Hardy's novel *The Mayor of Casterbridge*. There the procession and celebration is held in derision of an unpopular couple; this is still the practice in some North American communities, but in most cases the holding of a serenade does not indicate any lack of respect—in fact it may be a sign of popularity. The results of the enquiry into this word also indicate how a study of the present-day language may throw light on interesting local customs, which, like the words that denote them, frequently vary from place to place. Another by-product that may arise from such investigations consists of illuminating pieces of local folk-lore. Speech is often a key to the *mores* of the speakers.

Even a brief glance at the material already collected in this survey makes one doubtful about certain assumptions that are generally made with regard to present linguistic developments. First, the rate of change is very slow; rural speakers especially are much more conservative than most

[4] See M. H. Hanley, *"Serenade" in New England*, American Speech, April, 1933.

people think, in spite of the influence of the schools and other factors that tend towards the levelling of differences in speech. Secondly, hasty statements about the uniform pattern of North American life are not supported by an examination of the speech of this continent. The amount of variation between different communities and even between different individuals in the same community is astonishing. When we glance at the material collected for the three terms discussed above—*serenade, seesaw* and *earthworm*—we realize that although there may be standardization in our tooth-pastes and motor-cars, the more fundamental activity of human speech still reveals abundant variety and colour. It would be unfortunate if this should disappear.

We see that the story of our language does not close when we have investigated its past. The speech of the present takes on many forms and varying patterns. If our ears are alert and we cultivate our powers of observation we can detect all around us those signs of change that make language appear almost like a living organism with a capacity to survive and to adapt itself to a continually altering environment. Originally a crude and primitive means of communication, it has developed through the ages into a medium by which mankind can express the most profound emotions, the most subtle intellectual concepts, and the highest achievements of artistic creation.

APPENDIX A

GRIMM'S LAW

If the words on p. 39 are examined and compared certain definite similarities will emerge. The most striking of these are shown by the consonants *p, t, k* and *b, d, g*. Thus, if we compare Latin and English, we find that Lat. *p* appears regularly as *f* in the cognate Eng. word. One example can be seen in the table: Lat. *p*ater=Eng. *f*ather. To this may be added other cognates.

Latin	English
*p*isc(is)	*f*ish
*p*ed(em)	*f*oot
*p*ec(us) 'cattle'	*f*ee

Just as Lat. *p* is cognate with Eng. *f* so Lat. *t* is cognate with Eng. *th*. To the example already given—Lat. *t*res= Eng. *th*ree—may be added:

Latin	English
*t*u	*th*ou
men*t*(um) 'chin'	mou*th*
den*t*(em)	too*th*
fra*t*er	bro*th*er

Similarly the Lat. *k*-sound (spelt *c*) is equivalent to Eng. *h*.

Latin	English
*c*ord(is)	*h*eart
*c*an(is)	*h*ound
*c*ent(um)	*h*und(red)

An equally regular interchange is seen in the group *b, d, g*.

(1) Lat. *b* is equivalent to Eng. *p*.

Latin	English
labium	li*p*

(2) Lat. *d* is equivalent to Eng. *t*.

Latin	English
*d*uo	*t*wo
*d*ent(em)	*t*ooth
*d*omare	*t*ame
e*d*o	ea*t*
*d*ecem	*t*en
cor*d*(is)	hear*t*

(3) Lat. *g* is equivalent to Eng. *k(c)*.

Latin	English
*g*enu	*k*nee
*g*en(us)	*k*in
ju*g*um	yo*k*e
a*g*er	a*c*re

The same set of equivalents can be observed if Greek and English are compared.

A rather more complicated process is reflected in words which in Latin have *f* and *h*, in Greek *ph* (φ), *th* (θ) and *kh* (χ). These can be equated with the three sounds *b*, *d*, *g* in English. The following are examples:

Greek	Latin	English
*ph*ero (φέρω)	*f*ero	*b*ear
*ph*rater (φράτηρ)	*f*rater	*b*rother
*th*ura (θύρα)	(*f*oris)	*d*oor
*th*ugater (θυγάτηρ)		*d*aughter
*kh*ortos (χόρτος)	*h*ortus	*g*ard(en)

It will be noted that Gk. *th* (θ) is equivalent to Lat. *f*. We may now sum up these sound-equivalents as follows:

(1) Gk., Lat. *p, t, k*=Eng. *f, th, h*.

(2) Gk., Lat. *b, d, g*=Eng. *p, t, k*.

(3) Gk. *ph, th, kh* (Lat. *f, f, h*)=Eng. *b, d, g*.

These are part of a far-reaching system of equivalent sounds discovered in the Indo-European family of languages by two nineteenth-century linguists, the Danish Rasmus Rask and the German Jakob Grimm. It is usually called "Grimm's Law" after the latter scholar, one of the two brothers who collected *Grimm's Fairy Tales*. Similar parallels can be found between the consonants in cognate words belonging to other branches of the Indo-European family, and this series of regular resemblances is one of the most important proofs of the relationship between this large group of languages. The law was first formulated by Grimm in 1822.

Certain apparent exceptions to Grimm's Law were explained at a later date by another German, Karl Verner, and are stated in a supplementary rule known as Verner's Law.

We must be careful not to interpret Grimm's Law as meaning that Lat. *p* became Eng. *f*, etc. What is indicated is that Lat. *p* and Eng. *f* were both developed from the same sound in the parent Indo-European tongue and that this sound has taken a somewhat different direction in the two cognate languages. This holds good for the other equivalents as well.

We must also distinguish carefully between *cognate* words and *loan-words*. Cognate words are derived from the same ancestor; loan-words have been borrowed in historical times, sometimes quite recently, by one language from another. The cognate words will reflect the differences shown above, but if a word is borrowed, say from Latin by English, it will preserve the same sound as in Latin. Thus *frater* and *brother* are cognates, as shown by the *f* and *b*, while *fraternal* is a loan-word from Latin. Similarly *piscis* and *fish* are cognate, but *piscatorial* shows a direct borrowing. Compare also Lat. *dent(em)* =Eng. *tooth* (cognate) but *dental, dentist* (loan-words), Lat. *ped(em)* =Eng. *foot* (cognate) but *pedal, pedestrian* (loan-words).

APPENDIX B

Below are listed some of the chief variations between British and American spelling. The most striking feature of American spelling is the dropping of certain letters which are retained in British spelling. A large group of words in *–our* is affected. Some examples are:

Br. E.	Am. E.
colour	color
favour	favor
glamour	glamor (also glamour)
honour	honor
humour	humor
neighbour	neighbor
vigour	vigor

This variation is, however, not consistent. Br. E. uses the *–or* ending in certain words such as *horror, liquor, terror,* and Am. E. occasionally recognizes the *–our* form, e.g. *Saviour* by the side of *Savior, glamor* and *glamour.* In Br. E. the *u* is dropped in certain compounds of these words but retained in others; thus we find *humorous, humorist, glamorous, laborious, honorary, vigorous,* etc., but *honourable, favourable, labourite, labourer,* etc. In Am. E. the *–or* forms are found in all these words.

Another difference between the two systems of spelling is the doubling of *l* in Br. E. before certain endings, where Am. E. retains a single *l.* Some examples are:

Br. E.	Am. E.
levelled	leveled
revelled, reveller	reveled, reveler
travelled, traveller	traveled, traveler
councillor	councilor

counsellor	counselor
jewellery	jewelry
woollen	woolen

But in some words which have a single *l* in Br. E. *ll* is often found in Am. E., e.g.

Br. E.	Am. E.
fulfil	fulfil or fulfill
skilful	skilful or skillful

In a number of words Br. E. has *ae* or *oe*, which have been simplified to *e* in Am. E. Some examples are:

Br. E.	Am. E.
aesthetic, aesthete	esthetic, esthete
	(*ae* is also found)
mediaeval	medieval
diarrhoea	diarrhea
manoeuvre	maneuver

Other miscellaneous examples of simplification in Am. E. are:

Br. E.	Am. E.
axe	ax
catalogue, etc.	catalog
programme	program
mould	mold
moustache	mustache

In a group of words Br. E. has the ending *–re*, Am. E. *–er*. Some examples are:

Br. E.	Am. E.
centre	center
theatre	theater
metre	meter
fibre	fiber
manoeuvre	maneuver

In Br. E. *metre* and *meter* are used in different senses. This *–re* spelling is not consistent in Br. E.; cf. *neuter*. Br. E. has *–ce* in some words where Am. E. has *–se*, e.g.

Br. E.	Am. E.
defence	defense
offence	offense

But cf. Br. E. *offensive, defensive*.

Br. E. has *en–* in some words in which Am. E. has *in–*, e.g.

Br. E.	Am. E.
enclose	inclose
encrust	incrust
endorse	indorse
enquire	inquire
entrust	intrust

This difference, however, is not carried out consistently. A few miscellaneous differences are shown below:

Br. E.	Am. E.
cheque (on a bank)	check
for ever	forever
gaol (also jail)	jail
pedlar	ped(d)ler
pyjamas	pajamas
plough	plow
sceptic(al)	skeptic(al)
	(also *sc–*)
tyre	tire

Certain other more experimental Amer. spellings, e.g. *tho, thru, nite,* are not yet established, though their use seems to be spreading.

It should be noted that British dictionaries often include American spelling variants and American dictionaries often include British variants. There is a good deal of fluctuation in usage in individual writers.

ABBREVIATIONS

acc. accusative.
Am. E. (North) American English; see p. 173.
Amer. (North) American.
Br. British.
Br. E. British English; see p. 171.
cf. compare.
coll. colloquial.
dat. dative.
Du. Dutch.
e.g. for example.
E. Midl. East Midland; see p. 73.
Eng. English.
Fr. French.
gen. genitive.
Gen. Amer. General American; see p. 173.
Ger. German.
Gk. Greek.
Ital. Italian.
Lat. Latin.
lit. literary.
M.E. Middle English; see p. 33.
Mod. E. Modern English; see p. 33.
nom. nominative.
O.E. Old English; see p. 33.
O. Fr. Old French.
pron. pronounced.
Scand. Scandinavian.
S.O.D. Shorter Oxford Dictionary.
Sp. Spanish.
St. Eng. Standard English; see pp. 74, 172.
> develops into, becomes.
< is derived from, develops from.

BIBLIOGRAPHY

A. C. Baugh, *A History of the English Language*. Appleton-Century Co. (Ryerson Press)

L. V. Berrey and M. Van den Bark, *The American Thesaurus of Slang*. Crowell

L. Bloomfield, *Language*. Henry Holt & Co. (Clarke, Irwin)

H. Bradley, *The Making of English*. Henry Holt & Co. (Clarke, Irwin)

Sir W. A. Craigie, *Dictionary of American English*. Chicago University Press

Sir W. A. Craigie, *English Spelling: Its Rules and Reasons*. Crofts

G. O. Curme, *Grammar of the English Language*. D. C. Heath & Co. (Copp Clark)

O. F. Emerson, *The History of the English Language*. Macmillan

H. W. Fowler, *A Dictionary of Modern English Usage*. Oxford University Press

C. C. Fries, *The Structure of English*. Harcourt Brace & Co.

C. C. Fries, *The Teaching of the English Language*. Nelson

W. L. Graff, *Language and Languages*. Appleton-Century Co. (Ryerson Press)

J. S. Greenough and G. L. Kittredge, *Words and Their Ways in English Speech*. Macmillan

R. A. Hall, Jr., *Linguistics and Your Language*. Anchor Books (Doubleday)

H. W. Horwill, *A Dictionary of Modern American Usage*. Oxford University Press

A. Lloyd James, *Our Spoken Language*. Nelson

O. Jespersen, *Essentials of English Grammar*. Allen & Unwin (Nelson)

O. Jespersen, *Growth and Structure of the English Language*. Allen & Unwin (Nelson)

O. Jespersen, *Language, Its Nature, Development and Origin*. Allen & Unwin (Nelson)

D. Jones, *An English Pronouncing Dictionary*. E. P. Dutton & Co. (Smithers & Bonellie)

D. Jones, *An Outline of English Phonetics*. E. P. Dutton & Co. (Smithers & Bonellie)

A. G. Kennedy, *Bibliography of Writings on the English Language*. Yale University Press (Ryerson Press)

A. G. Kennedy, *Current English*. Ginn & Co.

J. S. Kenyon, *American Pronunciation*. Wahr

J. S. Kenyon and T. A. Knott, *A Pronouncing Dictionary of American English*. Merriam

H. Kokeritz, *Shakespeare's Pronunciation*. Yale University Press

G. P. Krapp, *The English Language in America*. Appleton-Century Co. (Ryerson Press)

G. P. Krapp, *The Pronunciation of Standard English in America*. Oxford University Press

T. R. Lounsbury, *A History of the English Language*. Henry Holt & Co. (Clarke, Irwin)

G. H. McKnight, *English Words and Their Background*. Appleton-Century Co. (Ryerson Press)

G. H. McKnight, *Modern English in the Making*. Appleton-Century Co. (Ryerson Press)

A. J. Marckwardt, *Introduction to the English Language*. Oxford University Press

M. M. Mathews, *A Dictionary of Americanisms*. Chicago University Press

H. L. Mencken, *The American Language*. A. A. Knopf, Inc. (Ryerson Press)

New English Dictionary, with its condensed versions such as *Shorter Oxford Dictionary*, *Concise Oxford Dictionary*, etc. Oxford University Press

H. C. O'Neill, etc., *A Guide to the English Language*. Nelson

E. Partridge, *British and American English Since 1900*. Dakers, London

E. Partridge, *A Dictionary of Slang*. George Routledge & Sons (Musson)

E. Partridge, *The World of Words*. Hamish Hamilton. Scribner

S. Potter, *Our Language*. Penguin Books

C. R. Quirk and C. L. Wrenn, *An Old English Grammar*. Methuen

S. Robertson and F. G. Cassidy, *The Development of Modern English*. Prentice-Hall

E. Sapir, *Language: An Introduction to the Study of Language*. Harcourt Brace & Co. (McClelland & Stewart)

E. Sapir, *Language: An Introduction to the Study of Speech*. Humphrey Milford

M. S. Serjeantson, *A History of Foreign Words in English*. Kegan Paul

L. P. Smith, *The English Language*. Henry Holt & Co. (Clarke, Irwin)

F. II. Vizitelly, *Essentials of English Speech and Literature*. Funk & Wagnalls Co. (Oxford University Press)

I. C. Ward, *The Phonetics of English*. W. Heffer & Sons (I. L. Hobden)

Webster's *Dictionary*

E. Weekley, *The English Language*. Jonathan Cape (Nelson)

E. Weekley, *The Romance of Words*. E. P. Dutton & Co. (Smithers & Bonellie)

H. Wentworth, *An American Dialect Dictionary*

H. Wentworth and S. B. Flexner, *Dictionary of American Slang.* Crowell

C. L. Wrenn, *The English Language.* Methuen

H. C. Wyld, *The Historical Study of the Mother Tongue.* E. P. Dutton & Co. (Smithers & Bonellie)

H. C. Wyld, *A Short History of English.* E. P. Dutton & Co. (Smithers & Bonellie)

Subject Index

Word Index